Holy Rise Up:
365 Days to Stand Bold in Faith

A Year of Strength, Courage, and Victory

Kelley McConnell

Crossroad to Healing Publishing

Holy Rise Up:
365 Days to Stand Bold in Faith

Scripture quotations taken from the Holy Bible, New International Version® NIV®.

Copyright © 1973, 1978, 1984, 2011 by Biblica, Inc.TM Used by permission. All rights reserved worldwide.

Published by Crossroad to Healing Publishing

For inquiries or permissions: crossroadtohealing@gmail.com

Printed in the United States of America
ISBN: 979-8-9938822-2-2

A Call to Rise

To the One Who Stands in Faith: _________________

With Strength and Prayer From: _________________

On this Day of Courage: _________________

This rise was meant to be shared, one step, one stand, one act of faith at a time.

May you walk strong in faith and live boldly in
God's victory.

Acknowledgments

To everyone who believed in this vision from the beginning, thank you.

To the men and young men who choose to stand firm and boldly in faith, even when the path is difficult. Your courage, honesty, and willingness to grow inspired the direction and spirit of every page of this devotional.

To my *Crossroad to Healing* community, for your prayers, encouragement, and testimonies that continue to reflect the strength found in God's truth. You remind me that transformation happens one step, one choice, one act of faith at a time.

To my family and friends, thank you for your patience, support, and grace as this book took shape page by page.

And above all, to God, the source of strength, truth, and victory. Every word in these pages belongs to Him. May He use this book to raise up hearts that stand boldly in faith.

Dedication

For those who stood beside me,
strengthened my faith,
and reminded me that
God calls us to rise.

To my parents,

Who taught me the value of hard work, discipline, and faith that stands steady over time. Through your example, kindness, and selfless support of others, you showed me what faithful strength and consistency look like. That foundation has carried me through every season and continues to lead me back to Christ, to truth, and to the calling God placed on my life. *Dad, you are the greatest man I've ever known.* You put others first without hesitation, carry a calm wisdom that sees beyond the surface, and have a way of warming hearts and making friends wherever you go.

To my husband, John

You have shown me what it looks like to believe without limits. Your determination, relentless work ethic, and refusal to give up have taught me that perseverance paired with faith can move mountains. You press forward with focus and creativity, finding solutions where others see obstacles. Your strength, vision, and steady belief remind me daily that our potential is far greater than we often realize.

To my children,
You are both a reflection of strength guided by compassion. Your determination and discipline are matched by kindness, empathy, and a genuine care for others. You lead with boldness, yet your hearts remain soft and loving, reminding me that true strength is found not only in achievement, but in how you love, serve, and show up for the world around you.

To my brother, Billy
You are one of the most generous people I know, and someone everyone can always count on. You have a rare way of lifting the spirit of those around you, and it's hard to find anyone who doesn't feel better after being in your presence. Your loyalty and ability to bring laughter into any room are a gift to everyone who knows you. You remind me that strength doesn't have to be heavy, and that kindness, humor, and presence can change the atmosphere wherever you go.

To Matt,
Our paths did not cross by chance. God has a way of connecting us with the people we are meant to learn from, walk alongside, and be strengthened by. Your courage, intelligence, and steadfast determination in the face of unthinkable circumstances have left a lasting mark on my life. You have shown me what it looks like to stand tall, keep faith steady, and move forward with hope even when the road is difficult. Your strength and example continue to remind me that faith, when lived with courage, can carry us farther than we ever expect.

To David,

You remind me that God is always at work, even in quiet and unexpected ways. Your courage, strength, and gentle spirit reflect a heart God is shaping with purpose and intention. Like the lion, there is a boldness within you that may not always roar, but carries great meaning and promise. I believe God has big plans for your life, and that He is leading you forward with care, courage, and love.

To Wesley,

Your life, though short, carried a depth of faith and wisdom far beyond your years. Knowing you strengthened my trust in God's goodness and reminded me that He writes every story with purpose. Your courage, joy, and quiet strength continue to point hearts toward Heaven and leave a mark that time cannot erase.

To my Crossroad to Healing community,

Every soul who has walked through my doors or shared a part of their story has shown me that true healing is built through faith, resilience, and courage.
And to every man and young man who will hold this book,
May these pages remind you that you were created for purpose, called to stand bold in faith, and equipped to rise in victory.
May this book always point hearts back to truth and call warriors to rise.
With gratitude and courage,
Kelley

For Leyton
The Strength That Rises Within

My sweet boy,

You are a living reminder that strength and tenderness were never meant to be separate. This book carries the same strength and heart I see in you.

You carry courage in your spirit, depth in your heart, and a steady determination that reflects God's hand on your life.

You see others. You make room for people. You lead not by force, but by kindness.

I watched you walk through a season that required more courage than most will ever know, and you did it with steadiness, faith, and bravery. You showed me that true strength is not loud or rushed, but formed through trust, endurance, and a heart anchored in God.

May you always walk boldly and lead with integrity. Your strength was placed within you by God Himself.

Stand firm. Rise strong. Walk faithfully with Jesus every step of the way. You are my pride, my prayer, and one of my greatest gifts.

Mom

"Be strong and courageous. Do not be afraid; do not be discouraged, for the Lord your God will be with you wherever you go."

Joshua 1:9

A Prayer of Dedication

Father God,

We place this work in Your hands.

Let these pages strengthen faith, sharpen discernment, and steady the hearts of those who read them.

May every word speak truth, every challenge build courage, and every reflection draw the reader closer to You.

When strength is tested, be their refuge. When fear rises, be their anchor. When the path is unclear, lead them forward in truth.

Use this devotional to form men and young men who stand firm in faith, walk in integrity, and rise in victory through Christ.

We give You all honor and authority.

In Jesus' Name, Amen.

"Be watchful, stand firm in the faith, act like men, be strong."

1 Corinthians 16:13

Introduction
Welcome to Your Holy Rise Up

A 365-Day Journey to Stand Bold in Faith, Strengthen Your Spirit, and Rise in Victory

You were never created to live timid, stay silent, or question who God called you to be. You were formed to stand firm, walk with courage, and rise with purpose.

Holy Rise Up is not about perfection or performance. It is about formation. The kind that happens when a man roots himself in truth, submits his strength to God, and learns to stand steady no matter the battle.

This devotional was written for men and young men who want more than surface-level faith. For those who are learning to lead, to endure, to heal, and to trust God in both victory and struggle.

Each day offers Scripture, a short reflection, affirmation and a Rise Up Challenge designed to help you live your faith with intention. Some days will be quiet and reflective. Others will call you to action. All are meant to build strength from the inside out. This is not a book to rush through. It is a guide to walk with you through a full year of growth, discipline, and faith in motion.

You will be reminded that strength and surrender are not opposites. That courage is built through obedience. And that true victory begins within.

Let this book meet you where you are and prepare you for where God is leading you.

Stand bold. Stay rooted. Rise in victory.

Here's to 365 days of standing firm: through faith, through obedience, through every season.

Your Holy Rise Up begins now.

How to Use This Book

There is no wrong way to begin your Holy Rise Up. You can start on any date, revisit meaningful days, or spend extra time in a phase that speaks to your season. This devotional is designed to meet you where you are and walk with you forward in faith.

Each day follows a steady rhythm:

Scripture • *Reflection* • *Affirmation* • *Rise Up Challenge*

Take your time.

Read with purpose.

Apply what God highlights.

Some days will call you to quiet reflection. Others will challenge you to act with courage and conviction.

Pause when needed, pray with intention,

and let God set the pace.

This journey is about commitment, consistency, and becoming the man God is forming you to be.

Table of Phases & Structure

A man of faith does not wait for strength to appear. He is shaped by God through obedience, endurance, and fire.

Phase 1: Rooted in Truth ● Establishing a firm foundation in Christ.

Theme: Identity, faith, surrender, spiritual grounding. Days: 1–73

Phase 2: Refined in Faith ● Allowing God to restore what has been tested and stretched.

Theme: Healing, repentance, forgiveness, inner renewal. Days: 74–130

Phase 3: Courage Under Fire ● Standing firm when pressure rises and faith is tested.

Theme: Courage, obedience, endurance, trust, God-given strength. Days: 131-174

Phase 4: Stand in Purpose ● Living boldly in your calling and walking out faith in action.

Theme: Leadership, obedience, courage, disciplined faith. Days: 175-234

Phase 5: Rise in Victory ● Walking forward with confidence, clarity, and restored strength.

Theme: Renewal, alignment, authority, spiritual maturity. Days: 235-365

Reflection & Renewal

At the end of each phase, you'll find brief moments for reflection and journaling. These pauses are intentional opportunities to assess your growth, acknowledge God's work, and prepare for what comes next with clarity.

Your Rise Up Flow

Scripture ● Reflection ● Affirmation ● Rise Up Challenge

Welcome to Your Holy Rise Up

You were never meant to live timid or uncertain. You were created to stand firm and rise through Him.

Dear Son of God,

If you're holding this book, it means something intentional has already begun. A decision to grow. A decision to strengthen your faith. A decision to become more grounded in who God created you to be.

The world often defines strength by performance, control, or power. But true strength is formed beneath the surface, where faith is tested, character is refined, and trust in God is built over time. Holy Rise Up is not about hype or surface-level belief. It is about consistency. Discipline. A faith that holds steady regardless of circumstance.

Over the next 365 days, you will walk through five intentional phases designed to strengthen your foundation, sharpen your faith, and prepare you to stand firm in every season.

Rooted in Truth: building an unshakable foundation of faith.

Refined in Faith: allowing God to shape character through discipline and trust.

Courage Under Fire: developing endurance, faithfulness, and resilience when faith is tested.

Stand in Purpose: stepping forward with confidence, conviction, and obedience.

Rise in Victory: walking in restored strength, clarity, and faith-led direction.

Each Day Offers a Simple Rhythm to

Build Strength from the Inside Out:

Scripture ● Reflection ● Affirmation ● Rise Up Challenge

You don't need to have everything figured out to begin. You simply

need to be willing to show up.

Each day is designed to help you build faith with intention, strength

through consistency, and discipline that carries into every area of

life.

Some days will challenge your thinking. Some will call you to

action. Others will ask you to stand firm and trust God in the

process. This is not about rushing or checking boxes. It's about

showing up daily and allowing God to shape you over time.

Growth happens one step at a time. Strength is built through

repetition. Faith deepens when you remain rooted.

Let this rhythm become part of your daily walk, a steady place

where truth anchors you and courage is renewed.

Your Holy Rise Up begins now.

With faith and conviction,

Kelley

Phase 1

Rooted in Truth

*Before you can rise, you must be
rooted in truth.*

Before you can rise, you must be rooted in truth.

This first phase of Holy Rise Up is about returning to your
foundation. The steady, unchanging truth of who God is and who
He created you to be. When you are rooted in truth, no storm can
shake you. No season can strip you of your purpose.

Being rooted means trusting what is solid, even when progress
feels slow. It is learning to listen for God's voice above the noise.
It is choosing truth over fear and conviction over comfort.
In this phase, allow God to draw you closer to His truth. Let Him
strengthen what is firm and expose what is false. Let truth
become the ground you stand on in every decision. Because
when truth runs deep, your faith becomes steady. Your strength
becomes consistent. And your rise becomes intentional.

Day 1
Intentional Roots

January 1

"They will be like a tree planted by the water that sends out its roots by the stream. It does not fear when heat comes; its leaves are always green."
Jeremiah 17:8

God planted you with intention. When pressure comes, you are not meant to break but to remain standing. Strength is built below the surface long before it is seen. Being rooted in truth keeps you steady through every season. Storms reveal the depth of your foundation, not your weakness.

Affirmation: I am rooted in God's truth and strengthened for every season.

Rise Up Challenge: Step outside today and pray, "Lord, keep me rooted in Your truth and firm in my faith."

Day 2
Truth Over Feelings

January 2

"Then you will know the truth, and the truth will set you free."
John 8:32

Feelings shift, but truth stands firm. When you build your life on God's Word instead of your emotions, you gain freedom that circumstances cannot take away.Truth does not change with the day. It anchors you when uncertainty tries to lead.

Affirmation: I live by God's truth, not my emotions.

Rise Up Challenge: When doubt surfaces today, say out loud, "God's truth leads me."

Day 3
Anchored Identity

January 3

"See what great love the Father has lavished on us,
that we should be called children of God."
1 John 3:1

Your worth is not earned through performance. It is secured through belonging. You lead best when you remember who you are and whose you are. Identity rooted in God cannot be shaken by opinion or failure.

Affirmation: I am a son of God, chosen and secure.

Rise Up Challenge: Look in the mirror and say, "I belong to God."

Day 4
Firm Foundation

January 4

"For no one can lay any foundation other than the one already laid, which is Jesus Christ."
1 Corinthians 3:11

Every strong life is built on something. When Christ is your foundation, storms may come, but collapse will not follow. What is built on truth stands when everything else falls.

Affirmation: My foundation is firm in Christ.

Rise Up Challenge: Identify one area of life you need to rebuild on God's truth and surrender it to Him.

Day 5
Unmoved by Pressure

January 5

"Be on your guard; stand firm in the faith; be courageous; be strong."
1 Corinthians 16:13

Pressure reveals what you are rooted in. Faith does not remove fear, but it gives you the strength to stand anyway.
Strength is choosing to remain steady when life presses hard.

Affirmation: I stand firm in faith under pressure.

Rise Up Challenge: When tension rises today, pause and pray, "God, strengthen me."

Day 6
Rooted in the Word

January 6

"Your word is a lamp for my feet, a light on my path."
Psalm 119:105

God's Word gives clarity when the path feels unclear. Truth does not just guide your steps, it guards your heart. Stay close to Scripture and you will not walk in darkness.

Affirmation: God's Word anchors my steps.

Rise Up Challenge: Read one Psalm today and let it steady your mind.

Day 7
Strength That Lasts

January 7

"Those who trust in the Lord are like Mount Zion,
which cannot be shaken."
Psalm 125:1

Lasting strength is not built quickly. God is forming endurance in you that will hold through every season. Trust grows deeper when you stay planted.

Affirmation: My strength is steady and enduring in God.

Rise Up Challenge: Thank God today for a challenge that strengthened you.

Day 8

Stillness is Strength

January 8

"The Lord will fight for you; you need only to be still."
Exodus 14:14

Stillness is an act of trust. When you release striving, you allow God to move on your behalf. Peace grows where control is released.

Affirmation: I trust God and remain steady in stillness.

Rise Up Challenge: Spend ten quiet minutes today without distractions and breathe deeply.

Day 9
Rooted in Integrity

January 9

"The righteous man walks in his integrity."
Proverbs 20:7

Integrity is consistency between belief and action. When your roots are grounded in truth, your life produces lasting influence. Character shapes legacy.

Affirmation: I walk in integrity and truth.

Rise Up Challenge: Choose truth today even when it costs you comfort.

Day 10
Built to Endure

January 10

"When the rain came down and the winds blew, it did not fall, because it had its foundation on the rock."
Matthew 7:25

Faith is proven under pressure. When your life is built on Christ, endurance becomes your testimony. You are not built to break. You are built to stand.

Affirmation: I am built to endure through Christ.

Rise Up Challenge: When life feels heavy today, say, "My foundation is firm."

Day 11

Rooted in Wisdom

January 11

*"The fear of the Lord is the beginning of wisdom,
and knowledge of the Holy One is understanding."*
Proverbs 9:10

Wisdom is not about knowing everything. It is about honoring God first. When you seek Him before opinions, clarity follows. A wise man listens more than he speaks and moves with discernment, not impulse.

Affirmation: God's wisdom guides every decision I make.

Rise Up Challenge: Before a decision today, pause and ask God for wisdom instead of reacting.

Day 12

Rooted in Faithfulness

January 12

"Let love and faithfulness never leave you; bind them around your neck, write them on the tablet of your heart."
Proverbs 3:3

Faithfulness is strength lived out daily. It is showing up when no one is watching and staying steady when progress feels slow. God honors men who keep their word because He always keeps His.

Affirmation: I remain faithful and steady in every season.

Rise Up Challenge: Follow through today on one commitment you have been tempted to delay.

Day 13

Rooted in Peace

January 13

*"Blessed is the man who trusts in the Lord,
whose confidence is in Him."*
Jeremiah 17:7

Peace does not come from control. It comes from confidence in God's hand. When trust runs deep, chaos loses its voice. A peaceful man carries calm into every space he enters.

Affirmation: My peace is firm because my trust is in the Lord.

Rise Up Challenge: Choose not to react to one situation today. Let peace guide your response.

Day 14

Rooted in Purpose

January 14

"For we are God's handiwork, created in Christ Jesus to do good works, which God prepared in advance for us to do."
Ephesians 2:10

You were made on purpose, for purpose. Every gift you carry and every battle you've faced has shaped you for a divine assignment. When you walk in purpose, you walk in strength.

Affirmation: I live with purpose and walk boldly in my calling.

Rise Up Challenge: Write down one area where you sense God calling you higher and pray for courage to respond.

Day 15

Stand Firm in Faith

January 15

"Therefore put on the full armor of God, so that when the day of evil comes, you may be able to stand your ground, and after you have done everything, to stand."
Ephesians 6:13

Standing firm is an active choice. Faith is built before pressure arrives, not during it. When you clothe yourself daily in God's truth, you are prepared to remain steady when challenges rise. God does not ask you to win every battle in your own strength. He asks you to stand, anchored in Him, trusting that He is your defense.

Affirmation: I stand firm and fearless in my faith.

Rise Up Challenge: Identify one area where you have been wavering and declare today that you will stand strong.

Day 16

Built on the Rock

January 16

"So this is what the Sovereign Lord says: 'See, I lay a stone in Zion, a tested stone, a precious cornerstone for a sure foundation; the one who relies on it will never be shaken.'"
Isaiah 28:16

When storms hit, your footing is revealed. Faith built on feelings collapses, but faith built on Christ stands unshaken. When Christ is your cornerstone, your strength does not depend on circumstances. What is built on Him will hold.

Affirmation: My foundation is unbreakable because it's built on the Rock.

Rise Up Challenge: Strengthen one spiritual habit today, prayer, Scripture, or worship, to reinforce your foundation.

Day 17

Rooted and Resilient

January 17

"Let your roots grow down into him, and let your lives be built on him."
Colossians 2:7

Deep roots weather any season. The secret of resilience isn't in avoiding wind; it's in holding fast to what's unseen. Staying connected to Him daily builds strength that lasts.

Affirmation: My roots reach deeper than any storm.

Rise Up Challenge: Write one truth about God that anchors you when life feels uncertain.

Day 18
Strength Through Surrender

January 18

"But he said to me, 'My grace is sufficient for you, for My power is made perfect in weakness.'"
2 Corinthians 12:9

God's strength flows where surrender begins. When you release control, you make space for His power to work in you. Grace sustains you when your own strength runs thin. Trust invites God to carry what you cannot.

Affirmation: My surrender makes room for God's strength.

Rise Up Challenge: Name one area you've been clinging to and hand it to God in prayer.

Day 19

Courage Over Comfort

January 19

"Have I not commanded you? Be strong and courageous. Do not be afraid; do not be discouraged, for the Lord your God will be with you wherever you go."
Joshua 1:9

Courage is choosing obedience even when fear lingers. God calls you forward because growth lives beyond comfort. When you trust His presence, you can move with confidence, knowing you are not alone.

Affirmation: I choose courage over comfort because God goes before me.

Rise Up Challenge: Take one bold step you've been delaying.

Day 20
Guard Your Heart

January 20

*"Above all else, guard your heart, for everything
you do flows from it."*
Proverbs 4:23

Your heart is a battlefield for belief. Protect what you let in, and
peace will guard what flows out. A heart aligned with truth and
produces steady strength.

Affirmation: I guard my heart with truth and discipline.

Rise Up Challenge: Audit what you consume. Replace one
thought, song, or voice with truth today.

Day 21
Faith in the Fire

January 21

"When you walk through the fire, you will not be burned; the flames will not set you ablaze."
Isaiah 43:2

Trials refine faith and reveal God's presence. Even in difficult seasons, He remains close and faithful. What you walk through does not define you. God's strength within you does.

Affirmation: I am refined, not destroyed, by the fire.

Rise Up Challenge: Reflect on one challenge that built your endurance and thank God for the strength it gave you.

Day 22

Discipline of the Lion

January 22

"For the Spirit God gave us does not make us timid, but gives us power, love and self-discipline."
2 Timothy 1:7

True strength includes restraint. Discipline directs power and keeps your life aligned with purpose. When you practice self-control, you honor what God is building within you.

Affirmation: I walk in disciplined power guided by God's Spirit.

Rise Up Challenge: Commit to one small discipline today, prayer at dawn, gratitude before bed, or silence before reaction.

Day 23
Rise After Failure

January 23

"The godly may trip seven times, but they will get up again."
Proverbs 24:16

Failure does not define you. Rising again is the proof of your faith. God's grace invites you forward, stronger and wiser than before.

Affirmation: I rise stronger every time I fall.

Rise Up Challenge: Write one lesson learned from a fall and how it fueled your growth.

Day 24
Anchored in Hope

January 24

*"We have this hope as an anchor for the soul, firm
and secure."*
Hebrews 6:19

Hope keeps you steady when progress feels slow. Trusting God's
promises anchors your heart through uncertainty. What God has
spoken remains firm, even when you cannot yet see the outcome.

Affirmation: My soul is anchored in unshakable hope.

Rise Up Challenge: Create a hope list of promises you're
standing on this season.

Day 25

Strength to Serve

January 25

"Whoever wants to become great among you must be your servant."
Matthew 20:26

True greatness isn't measured by power; it's shown through service. The strongest leaders kneel first. When you serve faithfully, God shapes your character and extends your influence.

Affirmation: My strength is revealed in service.

Rise Up Challenge: Serve someone quietly today, expecting nothing in return.

Day 26
Warrior of Peace

January 26

*"Blessed are the peacemakers, for they will be
called children of God."*
Matthew 5:9

Peace requires strength. Carrying calm into difficult spaces
reflects maturity and trust in God. When you choose peace, you
protect your spirit and honor His presence within you.

Affirmation: I fight battles with peace, not pride.

Rise Up Challenge: Respond to one tense moment with calm
instead of reaction.

Day 27
Faith That Finishes

January 27

"I have fought the good fight, I have finished the race, I have kept the faith."
2 Timothy 4:7

Finishing strong means staying faithful when the finish line is far. Lions don't stop halfway through the hunt.

Affirmation: I finish what faith started in me.

Rise Up Challenge: Complete one task you've been postponing as an act of perseverance.

Day 28
Rise in Righteousness

January 28

"The righteous are bold as a lion."
Proverbs 28:1

Boldness is your birthright when you walk in truth. When your heart is aligned with God, confidence follows naturally.

Affirmation: I rise with righteous boldness and roar with confidence in Christ.

Rise Up Challenge: Speak one truth boldly today, even if your voice trembles.

Day 29

Strong Tower

January 29

"The name of the Lord is a strong tower; the righteous run to it and are safe."
Proverbs 18:10

God is your refuge when life feels unstable. When life shakes, only what's built on Christ stands firm. Strength begins where self-reliance ends.

Affirmation: The Lord is my strong tower; I run to Him and I am safe.

Rise Up Challenge: Pray for God to reveal one area where you've relied on self instead of His strength.

Day 30
Wisdom That Leads

January 30

"If any of you lacks wisdom, you should ask God,
who gives generously to all without finding fault,
and it will be given to you."
James 1:5

True courage is guided by wisdom. The lion doesn't roar without reason; he moves with discernment. When you ask, He provides clarity.

Affirmation: I walk in holy wisdom that guards my path.

Rise Up Challenge: Pause before making a decision today and ask God for wisdom first.

Day 31
Steadfast in Truth

January 31

"Stand firm then, with the belt of truth buckled around your waist."
Ephesians 6:14

Truth is armor. When lies whisper, you tighten the belt and stand taller. A firm grip on truth keeps you steady in every season.

Affirmation: God's truth keeps me steady in every storm.

Rise Up Challenge: Speak one truth aloud today that silences fear.

Day 32

The Lion's Courage

February 1

"The Lord is my light and my salvation; whom shall I fear? The Lord is the stronghold of my life; of whom shall I be afraid?"
Psalm 27:1

Courage grows from confidence in God's presence. When you trust Him fully, fear loses its power. Boldness rises when faith leads your steps.

Affirmation: I am bold because God goes before me.

Rise Up Challenge: Do one thing today that fear has delayed.

Day 33
Sacred Stillness

February 2

"Be still, and know that I am God."
Psalm 46:10

Stillness builds awareness of God's work. Quiet moments strengthen trust and restore clarity. Lions know when to wait before they move.

Affirmation: My stillness is strength because God is working.

Rise Up Challenge: Set aside five silent minutes today to let peace lead you.

Day 34
Anchored Faith

February 3

"May the God of hope fill you with all joy and peace as you trust in him, so that you may overflow with hope by the power of the Holy Spirit."

Romans 15:13

Faith anchors you when life feels uncertain. Trusting God fills your heart with peace beyond understanding. Joy rises when you stand firm.

Affirmation: My faith holds fast in every tide.

Rise Up Challenge: Reflect on one time God kept you steady when life was uncertain.

Day 35

Iron Faith

February 4

"As iron sharpens iron, so one person sharpens another."
Proverbs 27:17

Strength grows through brotherhood. Faith forged with others becomes unbreakable. God uses community to refine and encourage you.

Affirmation: I sharpen and am sharpened by men of faith.

Rise Up Challenge: Encourage a friend in Christ today, remembering that iron strengthens iron.

Day 36
Unseen Roots

February 5

"He will have no fear of bad news; his heart is steadfast, trusting in the Lord."
Psalm 112:7

Roots grow where no one sees. Quiet trust beneath the surface builds lasting strength above it. Staying rooted in God prepares you for what lies ahead.

Affirmation: My confidence is planted deep in God's truth.

Rise Up Challenge: Thank God for a hidden season that strengthened your roots.

Day 37
Faithful Focus

February 6

*"Let your eyes look straight ahead; fix your gaze
directly before you."*
Proverbs 4:25

Distraction is the enemy of direction. Lions do not chase every
movement; they stay locked on purpose. Staying aligned with
God's purpose keeps distractions from pulling you off course.

Affirmation: My focus is fixed on the path God sets before me.

Rise Up Challenge: Remove one distraction that pulls you from
your mission today.

Day 38
Strength That Holds

February 7

"God is our refuge and strength, an ever-present help in trouble."
Psalm 46:1

Endurance is the quiet roar of faith. Storms reveal strength, not weakness. His presence brings stability when life feels heavy.

Affirmation: I endure because I am built on the Rock.

Rise Up Challenge: Face today's challenge with the mindset, "I'm grounded in truth."

Day 39
Heart of Honor

February 8

"Be devoted to one another in love. Honor one another above yourselves."
Romans 12:10

True strength serves. A heart of honor turns power into purpose. Leadership begins with a heart aligned with His values.

Affirmation: I lead with honor and strength of spirit.

Rise Up Challenge: Show quiet honor to someone who expects none.

Day 40
Peace That Reigns

February 9

"The Lord gives strength to His people; the Lord blesses His people with peace."
Psalm 29:11

Peace is a sign of God's rule within you. Strength and calm can exist together when trust runs deep. A lion at rest is still king. Let peace guide your responses.

Affirmation: Peace rules my heart because God reigns within me.

Rise Up Challenge: Respond calmly in one situation where anger usually wins.

Day 41
Truth in Action

February 10

"Do not merely listen to the word, and so deceive yourselves. Do what it says."
James 1:22

Truth takes root when it moves beyond words. Faith grows stronger when it is practiced daily through obedience and action. Living out God's Word builds strength that endures.

Affirmation: I am a doer of the Word, not a hearer only.

Rise Up Challenge: Live out one verse today through tangible action.

Day 42
Rooted and Rising

February 11

"So then, just as you received Christ Jesus as Lord, continue to live your lives in him, rooted and built up in him, strengthened in the faith as you were taught, and overflowing with thankfulness." Colossians 2:6–7

Growth comes from remaining grounded. Staying rooted in Christ allows strength to rise naturally over time. When your roots run deep in Christ, every new height stands on solid truth.

Affirmation: My strength and growth come from being rooted in Christ.

Rise Up Challenge: Write down one area of your life that's growing stronger because you've stayed grounded in faith.

Day 43
Faith That Holds

February 12

"The Lord is my rock, my fortress and my deliverer;
my God is my rock, in whom I take refuge."
Psalm 18:2

Faith becomes firm when it is tested. Strength rises from the ground of trust. He remains your refuge in every season.

Affirmation: My faith holds firm because God is my fortress.

Rise Up Challenge: When something shakes you today, stop and declare, "My God is my rock."

Day 44
Guided Steps

February 13

"The Lord makes firm the steps of the one who delights in Him."
Psalm 37:23

God directs the path of those who seek Him. Moving with patience allows His guidance to shape each step. Trust brings clarity as you walk forward.

Affirmation: My steps are ordered by the Lord.

Rise Up Challenge: Slow down today. Ask God to guide each move before you make it.

Day 45
Truth Over Noise

February 14

"The unfolding of your words gives light; it gives understanding to the simple."
Psalm 119:130

In a world full of noise, truth is still clear. Men of faith don't follow volume; they follow light. Staying close to His Word keeps your direction steady.

Affirmation: God's Word illuminates my path and keeps me steady.

Rise Up Challenge: Read one verse aloud and carry it in your heart all day.

Day 46
Stand Unmoved

February 15

"He alone is my rock and my salvation; He is my fortress, I will not be shaken."
Psalm 62:6

When faith is your foundation, no storm can sink you. Standing firm reflects trust in God's strength. Confidence grows from reliance on Him.

Affirmation: I will not be shaken because God is my fortress.

Rise Up Challenge: Breathe through challenge instead of reacting. Stand firm in peace.

Day 47
Strength in Obedience

February 16

"If you love Me, keep My commands."
John 14:15

Obedience reflects trust in God's wisdom. Choosing His way strengthens your faith and sharpens discernment. Faith grows when action follows belief.

Affirmation: I honor God through obedient faith.

Rise Up Challenge: Choose obedience over comfort in one small decision today.

Day 48
Honorable Ground

February 17

"The integrity of the upright guides them, but the unfaithful are destroyed by their duplicity."
Proverbs 11:3

Integrity is doing right when no one sees. It is the root system of honor. Walking in truth keeps your path secure.

Affirmation: My integrity is anchored in truth, not approval.

Rise Up Challenge: Keep a promise you've been tempted to delay or forget.

Day 49
Power in Prayer

February 18

"The prayer of a righteous person is powerful and effective."
James 5:16

Prayer is strength formed in silence. A lion roars in secret before he moves. Time with God prepares the ground for every victory.

Affirmation: My prayers carry power and purpose.

Rise Up Challenge: Pray boldly for someone else's victory today.

Day 50
The Root of Faithfulness

February 19

"Because of the Lord's great love we are not consumed, for his compassions never fail. They are new every morning; great is your faithfulness."
Lamentations 3:22–23

Faithfulness is strength expressed through consistency. Daily commitment builds trust with God and others. Remaining steady honors His promises.

Affirmation: I walk in faithful love and steadfast truth.

Rise Up Challenge: Finish a task you've started but left incomplete.

Day 51
Protected Within

February 20

"And the peace of God, which transcends all understanding, will guard your hearts and your minds in Christ Jesus."
Philippians 4:7

The heart is the core of courage. Guard it not with walls but with wisdom. When you trust God, peace settles even in uncertain moments.

Affirmation: My heart is protected by God's truth.

Rise Up Challenge: Identify one influence that weakens your peace and set a boundary.

Day 52
Rooted Perspective

February 21

"Set your minds on things above, not on earthly things."
Colossians 3:2

Perspective defines peace. Men who see through Heaven's lens walk differently on earth. Focusing on God's view keeps life aligned with purpose.

Affirmation: My mind stays aligned with God's view.

Rise Up Challenge: Trade one earthly distraction for a moment of spiritual focus today.

Day 53
Strength in Unity

February 22

"Though one may be overpowered, two can defend themselves. A cord of three strands is not quickly broken."
Ecclesiastes 4:12

Faith was never meant to walk alone. Strength multiplies in brotherhood. God uses unity to sharpen and sustain faith.

Affirmation: I am stronger with brothers who walk in faith.

Rise Up Challenge: Reach out to someone you trust and pray together this week.

Day 54
Firm in Faith

February 23

"So then, brothers and sisters, stand firm and hold fast to the teachings we passed on to you…"
2 Thessalonians 2:15

Courage grows through consistency and deepens faith. Holding to truth provides stability when pressures arise. Firm faith carries you forward.

Affirmation: I stand firm and fearless in faith.

Rise Up Challenge: When you feel pressure, say out loud, "I stand strong in Christ."

Day 55
Rooted in Grace

February 24

"Let us then approach God's throne of grace with confidence, so that we may receive mercy and find grace to help us in our time of need."
Hebrews 4:16

Confidence grows through reliance on His grace. God meets you with mercy when you draw near. True power is revealed when ego gives way to trust.

Affirmation: God's grace strengthens me where I am weak.

Rise Up Challenge: Admit a weak spot to God and invite His strength to fill it.

Day 56
Grounded in Purpose

February 25

"Being confident of this, that He who began a good work in you will carry it on to completion until the day of Christ Jesus."
Philippians 1:6

Purpose unfolds through faithfulness. God completes what He begins when you remain committed and present. Trusting His process keeps your steps aligned.

Affirmation: My purpose is God-designed and Spirit-driven.

Rise Up Challenge: Do one task today as an offering of excellence to God.

Day 57
Rooted in Strength

February 26

"The Lord is my strength and my shield; my heart trusts in Him, and He helps me."
Psalm 28:7

Strength rooted in faith cannot be shaken. When you trust God, your heart becomes unbreakable.

Affirmation: My strength is sustained by God's power.

Rise Up Challenge: Speak the words "I am strong in the Lord" three times today.

Day 58
Truth as Armor

February 27

"You are my hiding place and my shield; I hope in Your word."
Psalm 119:114

Truth protects the mind like armor. When the enemy whispers, the Word becomes your defense. His promises protect you.

Affirmation: God's truth guards my heart and mind.

Rise Up Challenge: Write down one scripture that silences your greatest fear.

Day 59
Rooted in Humility

February 28

"Humble yourselves, therefore, under God's mighty hand, that He may lift you up in due time."
1 Peter 5:6

Humility is the ground where honor grows. God raises those who kneel before Him. Trust grows through surrender.

Affirmation: I stay low so God can lift me higher.

Rise Up Challenge: Serve someone today without seeking credit or thanks.

Day 60
Faith That Builds

March 1

"By wisdom a house is built, and through understanding it is established."
Proverbs 24:3

Faith lays the foundation. Wisdom builds the walls. Every godly decision strengthens your structure. Each choice shapes what God is forming.

Affirmation: My faith builds a life that lasts.

Rise Up Challenge: Make one wise choice today that invests in your future.

Day 61
Rooted in Truthful Speech

March 2

"The Lord detests lying lips, but He delights in people who are trustworthy."
Proverbs 12:22

Your words reveal your roots. Truth spoken with grace builds trust that endures. Faithful speech honors God.

Affirmation: My words carry truth and strength.

Rise Up Challenge: Speak only what is true and uplifting today.

Day 62
Rooted in Faith Not Fear

March 3

"When I am afraid, I put my trust in You."
Psalm 56:3

Faith redirects fear. Trusting God steadies your heart when uncertainty arises. Courage is simply fear surrendered to God.

Affirmation: I walk in faith, not fear.

Rise Up Challenge: Face one thing you've been avoiding and trust God through it.

Day 63
Rooted in Hope

March 4

"Be strong and take heart, all you who hope in the Lord."
Psalm 31:24

Hope is the lion's heartbeat. It keeps you rising when the world wears you down. Staying hopeful fuels perseverance.

Affirmation: Peace is my default setting. God dwells within me.

Glow-Up Challenge: Take a slow, peaceful walk and thank God for every good thing you notice along the way.

Day 64
Rooted in Patience

March 5

"But those who wait on the Lord shall renew their strength; they shall mount up with wings like eagles."
Isaiah 40:31

Waiting builds trust. Patience allows God's timing to unfold with purpose. Renewal comes through stillness.

Affirmation: Patience renews my strength in God's timing.

Rise Up Challenge: Pause before you act today and ask, "Lord, is this Your timing?"

Day 65
Rooted in Character

March 6

"Do not be deceived: Bad company corrupts good character."
1 Corinthians 15:33

The character is tested by company. Surround yourself with those who sharpen your faith. Choose wisely who walks beside you.

Affirmation: My character reflects Christ in all I do.

Rise Up Challenge: Spend time with someone who strengthens your walk with God.

Day 66
Running with Endurance

March 7

"Let us run with perseverance the race marked out for us."
Hebrews 12:1

Starting takes energy; finishing takes faith. Stay the course God set for you. Endurance grows through commitment. Staying faithful keeps you moving forward. Finish what God has placed before you.

Affirmation: I persevere through faith, not feelings.

Rise Up Challenge: Complete something you've left unfinished.

Day 67
Rooted in Peace Under Pressure

March 8

"Peace I leave with you; my peace I give you. I do not give to you as the world gives."
John 14:27

When you carry Christ within, pressure cannot break you. Peace remains steady. Trusting God calms the heart. His presence guards your spirit.

Affirmation: My peace comes from the Prince of Peace.

Rise Up Challenge: When stress hits, pause and say, "Peace is still mine."

Day 68
Rooted in Purpose Over Pride

March 9

"Commit to the Lord whatever you do, and He will establish your plans."
Proverbs 16:3

Purpose aligns your plans with God's will. When you commit your path, He secures your steps. Commitment invites His guidance. Trust shapes success.

Affirmation: My plans succeed because they belong to God.

Rise Up Challenge: Surrender a goal to God today and trust His direction.

Day 69
Rooted in Truth Through Testing

March 10

"Consider it pure joy, my brothers and sisters, whenever you face trials of many kinds, because you know that the testing of your faith produces perseverance."
James 1:2–3

Testing strengthens and reveals roots. Faith deepens through pressure and persistence. Growth follows endurance.

Affirmation: My faith grows stronger under testing.

Rise Up Challenge: Thank God for a trial that has made you wiser.

Day 70
Rooted in Gratitude

March 11

*"Give thanks in all circumstances; for this is
God's will for you in Christ Jesus."*
1 Thessalonians 5:18

Gratitude keeps your roots hydrated with joy. Thankful hearts
grow stronger every season. Faith grows through appreciation.

Affirmation: I am grateful in every circumstance.

Rise Up Challenge: List three things you're thankful for before
you sleep.

Day 71
Rooted in Truthful Living

March 12

"Whoever walks in integrity walks securely, but whoever takes crooked paths will be found out."
Proverbs 10:9

When you walk upright, you walk unafraid. Integrity brings security. Living honestly strengthens confidence and peace. Truth guides your steps.

Affirmation: My life reflects truth in every step.

Rise Up Challenge: Do the right thing today even if no one sees it.

Day 72
Rooted in Resilience

March 13

"We are hard pressed on every side, but not crushed; perplexed, but not in despair."
2 Corinthians 4:8

Resilience is faith that refuses to quit. You bend but you don't break because God holds your core. Strength remains firm.

Affirmation: I am resilient in Christ.

Rise Up Challenge: When you feel weary, say aloud, "I am pressed but not crushed."

Day 73
Rooted in Truth,
Ready to Rise

March 14

*"Now the Lord is the Spirit, and where the Spirit of
the Lord is, there is freedom."*
2 Corinthians 3:17

Freedom flows from truth. You've built your foundation; now it's time to rise boldly in faith. Your foundation is secure.

Affirmation: I am rooted in truth and rising in freedom.

Rise Up Challenge: Write one sentence about how truth has changed your life this season.

Phase 1
Reflection
Rooted in Truth

Take a breath, warrior of faith.

You've done more than read words on a page; you've built roots that reach deep into the ground of God's truth.

This phase wasn't about appearance or performance. It was about foundation. You've learned that strength doesn't come from striving but from standing. In Scripture. In conviction. In faith when the world shifts.

Your roots are no longer shallow. They're steady. They drink from living water. You've anchored your identity not in what changes, but in Who never does.

Every man of God begins here, not with the roar but with the rooting. What's grown quietly beneath the surface will soon rise in strength and courage.

You are becoming unshakable. You are grounded in grace. You are Rooted in Truth.

Where in my life have I seen my faith become stronger and more grounded?

What truths from Scripture have reshaped the way I see myself or my purpose?

What roots do I still need to strengthen before moving forward?

How will I stay anchored when challenges test my foundation?

Prayer

Lord, thank You for planting my feet in Your truth. Thank You for teaching me to stand when the ground around me shakes. Let my faith remain rooted and unmovable. Strengthen my mind, guard my heart, and help me rise in courage and conviction.

In Jesus' name, Amen.

Affirmation

I am rooted in Christ, grounded in truth, and prepared to rise.

Phase 2

Refined in Faith

"Now that your roots have taken hold in truth, it is time to let God strengthen the faith that will carry you forward."

This is where strength meets surrender. Every warrior must walk through the fire to discover what his faith is truly made of. This phase is not about breaking you; it is about building you. Refinement removes what is weak so that what is pure can remain.

You have been planted in truth, and now God begins shaping your endurance. It is here that faith becomes less about what you say and more about how you stand. It is here that trust becomes muscle and obedience becomes armor.

The refining fire may test your patience, your pride, or your peace, but remember that gold only shines after the heat. This is where you learn that surrender is not defeat. It is strength under divine command.

Day 74
Strength in the Fire

March 15

"But He knows the way that I take; when He has tested me, I will come forth as gold."
Job 23:10

Faith grows stronger in the furnace. God doesn't test to break you but to build endurance. The pressure you feel is producing something precious that cannot be shaken.

Affirmation: I am being refined, not reduced. God is forging strength in me.

Rise Up Challenge: Reflect on a time when struggle shaped your character and thank God for the growth.

Day 75
Stand Firm

March 16

"Stand firm, and you will win life."
Luke 21:19

Faith isn't passive. It stands its ground when the wind blows hardest. God calls you to hold your position, not through pride, but through conviction anchored in His Word.

Affirmation: I stand firm in faith, fearless in the face of adversity.

Rise Up Challenge: When you feel shaken today, pause and declare aloud, "I will not be moved."

Day 76
Obedience in the Battle

March 17

"If you are willing and obedient, you will eat the good things of the land."
Isaiah 1:19

Refinement happens when obedience meets pressure. God rewards the man who chooses His voice over comfort. Obedience is the warrior's greatest weapon.

Affirmation: My obedience invites God's best into my life.

Rise Up Challenge: Follow through today on one thing you've been delaying in faith.

Day 77
Faith That Endures

March 18

"Let perseverance finish its work so that you may be mature and complete, not lacking anything."
James 1:4

Endurance isn't built in ease but in challenge. Every trial is strength training for your spirit. Let the process finish its work; your maturity depends on it.

Affirmation: I endure with purpose. God is completing His good work in me.

Rise Up Challenge: Don't rush what God is refining. Write one area where He's teaching you patience.

Day 78
Trust Through the Heat

March 19

"The crucible is for silver and the furnace is for gold, and the Lord tests hearts."
Proverbs 17:3

Fire doesn't destroy those who walk with God. It defines them. You are not walking alone through the flames; His presence is your protection.

Affirmation: I walk through every fire with God beside me.

Rise Up Challenge: Each time pressure rises today, whisper, "God is with me."

Day 79
Quiet Confidence

March 20

"In repentance and rest is your salvation, in quietness and trust is your strength."
Isaiah 30:15

Stillness is not weakness; it's trust in motion. Faith doesn't always fight with fists but sometimes with quiet confidence that God is already at work.

Affirmation: My stillness is strength because God fights for me.

Rise Up Challenge: Spend five minutes in silence today, releasing control and resting in His power.

Day 80
Purified Purpose

March 21

"Create in me a pure heart, O God, and renew a steadfast spirit within me."
Psalm 51:10

Refinement begins in the heart. God removes impurities not to shame you but to restore you. A purified heart beats with holy purpose.

Affirmation: My heart is clean, and my purpose is clear.

Rise Up Challenge: Pray for God to renew your motives and align them with His mission.

Day 81
The Power of Humility

March 22

"Humble yourselves before the Lord, and He will lift you up."
James 4:10

Humility doesn't weaken a man; it strengthens him. God promotes those who bow low before His will. True warriors kneel before they rise.

Affirmation: I rise by bowing before God. Humility is my honor.

Rise Up Challenge: Choose humility today in one area where pride usually leads.

Day 82
The Test of Faith

March 23

"Without faith it is impossible to please God."
Hebrews 11:6

God doesn't ask for flawless performance, only faith that endures. Every test is an opportunity to prove that you trust His unseen hand.

Affirmation: My faith pleases God even when I cannot see the outcome.

Rise Up Challenge: Step out today in one small act of faith without full clarity.

Day 83
Patience in the Process

March 24

*"Wait for the Lord; be strong and take heart and
wait for the Lord."*
Psalm 27:14

Refinement is rarely fast. God's best work takes time. Patience is
proof that you trust His timing more than your own.

Affirmation: I wait well. My faith is steady while God works in
silence.

Rise Up Challenge: Practice patience today when plans don't
move at your pace.

Refined in Faith

Day 84
Strength to Forgive

March 25

"Then Peter came to Jesus and asked, 'Lord, how many times shall I forgive my brother or sister who sins against me?' Jesus answered, 'I tell you, not seven times, but seventy-seven times.'"
Matthew 18:21–22

Forgiveness is refinement for the soul. It takes strength to let go of what wounded you, but freedom always follows forgiveness.

Affirmation: I release what no longer serves me and walk free in forgiveness.

Rise Up Challenge: Write the name of one person you need to forgive and pray for peace over them.

Day 85
Refining Your Focus

March 26

"Set your minds on things above, not on earthly things."
Colossians 3:2

Refined faith is focused faith. Distraction dulls your spirit, but focus sharpens it. Keep your eyes fixed on eternity, not the temporary noise.

Affirmation: My focus is fixed on God's purpose, not my problems.

Rise Up Challenge: Eliminate one distraction today that keeps you from clear focus on God.

Day 86
Peace in Pressure

March 27

"You will keep in perfect peace those whose minds are steadfast, because they trust in you."
Isaiah 26:3

Pressure doesn't have to steal your peace. Refinement teaches calm under fire. God's peace guards you while the world watches how you endure.

Affirmation: I am calm under pressure because Christ guards my heart.

Rise Up Challenge: When tension builds today, take one deep breath and whisper, "Your peace is my strength."

Day 87
Faith That Finishes Strong

March 28

"Run in such a way as to get the prize."
1 Corinthians 9:24

Refined faith doesn't fizzle out; it finishes. The battle may be long, but the victory belongs to the one who refuses to quit.

Affirmation: I finish what God starts in me. My endurance honors Him.

Rise Up Challenge: Look back on something you persevered through and thank God for your finishing strength.

Day 88
The Strength of Discipline

March 29

"No discipline seems pleasant at the time, but painful. Later on, however, it produces a harvest of righteousness and peace for those who have been trained by it."
Hebrews 12:11

Discipline shapes devotion. The man who submits to correction becomes unshakable. What feels restrictive now will yield strength that lasts.

Affirmation: My discipline today builds my strength for tomorrow.

Rise Up Challenge: Commit to one consistent discipline this week that strengthens your faith or character.

Day 89
Rooted in Perseverance

March 30

"Blessed is the one who perseveres under trial because, having stood the test, that person will receive the crown of life that the Lord has promised to those who love Him."
James 1:12

Perseverance proves love. When you refuse to quit, Heaven takes notice. Every test is an opportunity to choose endurance over escape.

Affirmation: I persevere through trials knowing God's reward is sure.

Rise Up Challenge: Reflect on one challenge that stretched you and thank God for how it strengthened your resolve.

Day 90
Strength in Surrender

March 31

"The Lord is close to the brokenhearted and saves those who are crushed in spirit."
Psalm 34:18

Surrender is not weakness; it is wisdom. God restores what you lay down. When you stop fighting in your own strength, you make room for His power to move.

Affirmation: My surrender invites God's victory.

Rise Up Challenge: Release one burden to God today through prayer, and trust Him to carry it.

Day 91
The Power of Prayer

April 1

*"Call to me and I will answer you and tell you
great and unsearchable things you do not know."*
Jeremiah 33:3

Prayer isn't a last resort; it's your first line of battle. When you pray, Heaven listens, and hell trembles. Prayer aligns your heart with divine strength.

Affirmation: My prayers carry power because they are rooted in righteousness.

Rise Up Challenge: Take ten minutes today to pray intentionally over your next step or decision.

Day 92
Refining Through Resistance

April 2

"We also glory in our sufferings, because we know that suffering produces perseverance."
Romans 5:3

Resistance builds resilience. The challenges that frustrate you now are the very ones forming your faith. Rejoice in the refining, for it proves your strength.

Affirmation: I grow stronger through resistance. My faith thrives under pressure.

Rise Up Challenge: When something frustrates you today, thank God for the growth hidden within it.

Day 93
Strength in Service

April 3

"The greatest among you will be your servant."
Matthew 23:11

The true mark of leadership is service. When you serve others with humility, you reflect the heart of Christ. Greatness is found in giving, not gaining.

Affirmation: I lead through serving. My strength is found in humility.

Rise Up Challenge: Serve someone quietly today without recognition. Let kindness be your reward.

Day 94
Faith Under Pressure

April 4

"The Lord is my strength and my defense; He has become my salvation."
Psalm 118:14

Pressure reveals what's real. You might bend, but you will not break when your foundation is Christ. Every challenge becomes proof of your endurance.

Affirmation: I am restored from the inside out. God is making all things new in me.

Glow-Up Challenge: Reflect on how you've changed since starting this phase. Write one word that defines your restoration so far.

Day 95
The Purity of Purpose

April 5

"Blessed are the pure in heart, for they will see God."
Matthew 5:8

A pure heart keeps your vision clear. God reveals direction to those whose motives are aligned with His truth. Purity brings clarity to purpose.

Affirmation: My heart is pure, and my purpose rises clear before God.

Rise Up Challenge: Before any decision today, pause and ask, "Is my motive pure?"

Day 96
Steadfast Spirit

April 6

"Therefore, my dear brothers and sisters, stand firm. Let nothing move you. Always give yourselves fully to the work of the Lord."
1 Corinthians 15:58

Steadfastness is silent strength. Faith doesn't waver when it knows who holds the future. Stay faithful in your work; God sees your consistency.

Affirmation: I remain steadfast in faith and committed to my calling.

Rise Up Challenge: Finish one task today with excellence as an offering to God.

Day 97
Refined Perspective

April 7

"We fix our eyes not on what is seen, but on what is unseen, since what is seen is temporary, but what is unseen is eternal."
2 Corinthians 4:18

Faith shifts your focus. The refining process changes how you see the world. What feels painful now may be preparing eternal purpose later.

Affirmation: My eyes are fixed on what lasts. I see through God's eternal lens.

Rise Up Challenge: When frustration rises, say, "This is temporary, but God's purpose is eternal."

Day 98
Tested and True

April 8

"The Lord examines the righteous, but the wicked, those who love violence, He hates."
Psalm 11:5

Tests don't come to expose your weakness but to affirm your worth. Every test is proof that God trusts you to stand under pressure.

Affirmation: I am tested and found faithful. My trials prove my trust in God.

Rise Up Challenge: Reflect on one test you've passed with faith and record what it taught you.

Day 99
The Strength of Hope

April 9

*"Why, my soul, are you downcast? Put
your hope in God."*
Psalm 42:11

Hope is holy fuel. When others faint, hope keeps you moving
forward. Waiting on God renews your power to rise.

Affirmation: My hope in God restores my strength and lifts my
spirit.

Rise Up Challenge: Write down one area where you feel weary
and declare hope over it today.

Day 100
Refined Courage

April 10

"Be strong and courageous. Do not be afraid... for the Lord your God goes with you."
Deuteronomy 31:6

Courage does not roar. It remains. When fear whispers, faith stands taller. God refines your courage through every step of trust you take.

Affirmation: I walk boldly because my courage is anchored in God.

Rise Up Challenge: Take one step today that fear has delayed.

Day 101
Faith That Rebuilds

April 11

"Unless the Lord builds the house, the builders labor in vain."
Psalm 127:1

What God tears down, He intends to rebuild stronger. Faith rebuilds not by striving, but by surrendering the blueprint back to Him.

Affirmation: God rebuilds what I surrender. My foundation stands firm in Him.

Rise Up Challenge: Identify one area of life that needs rebuilding and invite God to take over the design.

Day 102
Fire-Proof Faith

April 12

*"These trials will show that your faith is genuine. It
is being tested as fire tests and purifies gold."*
1 Peter 1:7

Fire-proof faith doesn't fear the flames. It glows brighter in the
heat. Every trial purifies your trust until only what's real remains.

Affirmation: My faith is genuine and resilient under fire.

Rise Up Challenge: Write a short prayer thanking God for the
strength you've gained through past trials.

Day 103
Faith in the Furnace

April 13

*"Dear friends, do not be surprised at the fiery ordeal
that has come on you to test you, as though something
strange were happening to you."*
1 Peter 4:12

Refinement isn't comfortable, but it's never wasted. Every flame
that tests you also forges you. The same God who allows the fire
stands beside you in it.

Affirmation: I am protected and purified by God's presence in
every trial.

Rise Up Challenge: Think of one area where you feel tested.
Thank God for the fire that is forging your faith.

Day 104
The Anchor of Peace

April 14

*"He grants peace to your borders and satisfies
you with the finest of wheat."*
Psalm 147:14

Peace is not the absence of battle but the anchor in it. When you are rooted in God's strength, storms cannot sink you.

Affirmation: My peace is anchored in God's strength alone.

Rise Up Challenge: Pause three times today to breathe deep and speak, "My peace comes from You, Lord."

Day 105
Endurance
Through Faith

April 15

*"Let us run with perseverance the race marked out
for us, fixing our eyes on Jesus."*
Hebrews 12:1–2

Endurance is the evidence of faith. When your focus stays on
Christ, you can press forward through any terrain.

Affirmation: I run my race with focus and faith.

Rise Up Challenge: When you feel tired today, pause and
whisper, "My eyes are on You, Jesus."

Day 106
Refined Integrity

April 16

*"Better is the poor who walks in his integrity than
one perverse in his ways."*
Proverbs 19:1

Integrity is what you choose when no one is watching. It is the core of refined character. Honesty builds a reputation that God can use.

Affirmation: My integrity is my strength. I walk truthfully before God and man.

Rise Up Challenge: Be truthful in one small moment where it would be easier to hide.

Day 107
Faith That Waits

April 17

"The Lord is good to those whose hope is in him, to the one who seeks him; it is good to wait quietly for the salvation of the Lord."
Lamentations 3:25–26

Waiting is not wasted time. It's training time. Faith matures in the quiet places where you learn to trust without proof.

Affirmation: I am patient and peaceful in God's timing.

Rise Up Challenge: When impatience rises today, breathe and say, "I trust Your timing, Lord."

Day 108
The Refiner's Hand

April 18

"He will sit as a refiner and purifier of silver."
Malachi 3:3

God's refining is never random. He knows what to remove and what to reveal. You are being polished for purpose.

Affirmation: God's refining makes me shine for His glory.

Rise Up Challenge: List one thing God has removed from your life that made room for growth.

Day 109
Rooted Courage

April 19

"The Lord is with me; I will not be afraid. What can mere mortals do to me?"
Psalm 118:6

Courage is a command, not a suggestion. When you remember who walks with you, fear loses its grip.

Affirmation: My courage is anchored in God's presence.

Rise Up Challenge: Face one thing you've been avoiding and step forward in faith.

Day 110
Faith That Fights

April 20

"Fight the good fight of the faith. Take hold of the eternal life to which you were called."
1 Timothy 6:12

Standing for truth will cost you comfort at times. But every step of obedience builds strength in your spirit. The Lord fights beside you and within you.

Affirmation: I fight the good fight with divine strength and courage.

Rise Up Challenge: Pray for boldness to stand firm for truth today, even when it's unpopular.

Day 111
Strength Through Humility

April 21

"Humility comes before honor."
Proverbs 15:33

Humility is not weakness. It's surrendered strength. The lower you bow before God, the higher He can lift you.

Affirmation: My humility honors God and strengthens my spirit.

Rise Up Challenge: Choose a moment to serve quietly today without seeking recognition.

Day 112
The Fire of Obedience

April 22

"To obey is better than sacrifice."
1 Samuel 15:22

Obedience keeps you in alignment with Heaven's flow. Sacrifice without surrender is noise; obedience is power.

Affirmation: I choose obedience over appearance.

Rise Up Challenge: Follow through on one prompt God has placed on your heart.

Day 113
Refined Vision

April 23

"Open my eyes that I may see wonderful things in your law."
Psalm 119:18

Faith sharpens your vision when you walk by God's word. Each step you take in light makes the next clearer.

Affirmation: God's word guides my path and clarifies my purpose.

Rise Up Challenge: Read one chapter of Scripture tonight and ask, "What is God illuminating for me?"

Day 114
The Strength of Patience

April 24

"But if we hope for what we do not yet have, we wait for it patiently."
Romans 8:25

Patience is faith in motion. It is the quiet confidence that God's timing is always perfect.

Affirmation: I wait with faith and walk with peace.

Rise Up Challenge: When delays come today, say, "Your timing, Lord, not mine."

Day 115
The Refinement of Forgiveness

April 25

"Be kind and compassionate to one another, forgiving each other, just as in Christ God forgave you."
Ephesians 4:32

Forgiveness frees you from chains that can't be seen. Refined faith does not hold grudges; it hands them to God.

Affirmation: I am free because I forgive.

Rise Up Challenge: Pray for someone you've struggled to forgive and release them to God.

Day 116
Refined Identity

April 26

"Therefore, if anyone is in Christ, the new creation has come: The old has gone, the new is here!"
2 Corinthians 5:17

Refinement is not just removing impurities. It reveals who you truly are. You are no longer defined by failure but by faith.

Affirmation: I am a new creation, refined and restored in Christ.

Rise Up Challenge: Write down three truths about who you are in Christ and speak them out loud today.

Day 117
Enduring Faith

April 27

"Let us not become weary in doing good,
for at the proper time we will reap a
harvest if we do not give up."
Galatians 6:9

Enduring faith is forged through focus. When the world wavers, you remain steady because your roots run deep in truth.

Affirmation: I stand firm and unshaken, rooted in strength and faith.

Rise Up Challenge: When distractions pull, pause and say, "I'm standing firm in You, Lord."

Day 118
The Power of Perspective

April 28

"Whatever is true, whatever is noble, whatever is right, whatever is pure, whatever is lovely, whatever is admirable, if anything is excellent or praiseworthy, think about such things."
Philippians 4:8

Perspective refines purpose. When your thoughts rise higher, your worries shrink smaller. Faith fixes its eyes on what lasts.

Affirmation: My mind is set on heavenly things; peace rules my thoughts.

Rise Up Challenge: Redirect one anxious thought upward today with a verse or prayer.

Day 119
Refined By Grace

April 29

"For it is by grace you have been saved through faith, and this is not from yourselves; it is the gift of God."
Ephesians 2:8

Grace turns weakness into witness. Every shortcoming is a setup for God's strength to shine through you.

Affirmation: God's grace perfects my strength.

Rise Up Challenge: Name one weakness and thank God for how His grace redeems it.

Day 120
Faith That Speaks Life

April 30

"The tongue has the power of life and death, and those who love it will eat its fruit."
Proverbs 18:21

Your words shape your world. Refined faith learns to speak what aligns with Heaven, not fear.

Affirmation: I speak life and truth; my words carry faith.

Rise Up Challenge: Replace every negative word today with one of faith and encouragement.

Day 121
The Strength
of Stillness

May 1

"Be still before the Lord and wait patiently for Him."
Psalm 37:7

Stillness is strength in disguise. Faith doesn't always move mountains; sometimes it waits beside them with peace.

Affirmation: My stillness is power; I rest in God's presence.

Rise Up Challenge: Spend five quiet minutes today doing nothing but breathing in His peace.

Refined in Faith

Day 122
Faith That Focuses

May 2

"Turn my eyes away from worthless things;
preserve my life according to Your word."
Psalm 119:37

Focus is refinement in motion. What you fix your eyes on forms your future. Keep your gaze on God, and clarity will follow.

Affirmation: My focus is holy; my direction is clear.

Rise Up Challenge: Fast from one small distraction today and redirect that time to prayer.

Day 123
Refined Through Love

May 3

"Do everything in love."
1 Corinthians 16:14

Love refines motive. Strength without love is pride; love turns power into purpose.

Affirmation: I move in love, and it strengthens everything I do.

Rise Up Challenge: Do one act of love today without expecting anything in return.

Day 124
Faith That Forgives

May 4

""If you forgive other people when they sin against you, your heavenly Father will also forgive you."
Matthew 6:14

Forgiveness frees the fighter's heart. Letting go is not losing. It is releasing yourself into peace.

Affirmation: I forgive freely and live fully.

Rise Up Challenge: Write down one name or memory you're releasing to God today.

Day 125
Strength Through Trust

May 5

*"Trust in the Lord with all your heart and
lean not on your own understanding."*
Proverbs 3:5–6

Trust is the backbone of refined faith. When understanding
fails, trust steps forward.

Affirmation: I trust God completely; He leads my every step.

Rise Up Challenge: When worry surfaces, repeat, "I lean on
Your wisdom, not mine."

Day 126
Refined By Fire

May 6

*"The Lord will be a wall of fire around it,
and I will be its glory within."*
Zechariah 2:5

Fire doesn't destroy the faithful; it defines them. The presence of God protects even in the heat of refining.

Affirmation: God surrounds me with His fire and fills me with His glory.

Rise Up Challenge: Pray for courage to stand firm when life feels like the furnace.

Day 127
Faith That Carries Through

May 7

"May you be strengthened with all power, according to his glorious might, so that you may have great endurance and patience."
Colossians 1:11

Faith starts strong and finishes well. What God begins, He perfects through perseverance.

Affirmation: I finish strong because God finishes His work in me.

Rise Up Challenge: Complete one unfinished task today as an act of obedience.

Day 128
Strength In Community

May 8

*"Two are better than one, because they have
a good return for their labor."*
Ecclesiastes 4:9

Refinement thrives in relationship. Brotherhood strengthens
belief. True faith grows when sharpened by others who walk
the same road.

Affirmation: I am strengthened through godly connection.

Rise Up Challenge: Encourage a brother in faith today with a
call or message.

Day 129
Refined Conviction

May 9

"Do not conform to the pattern of this world, but be transformed by the renewing of your mind."
Romans 12:2

Conviction separates strength from compromise. A renewed mind resists conformity and walks in courage.

Affirmation: My convictions are clear, my faith unmoved.

Rise Up Challenge: Stand by one godly value today even if it costs comfort.

Day 130
Faith That Glorifies God

May 10

*"Let your light shine before others, that
they may see your good deeds and glorify
your Father in heaven."*
Matthew 5:16

Refined faith points upward. Every act of courage,
kindness, and endurance becomes a mirror of His glory.

Affirmation: My life shines for God's glory alone.

Rise Up Challenge: Do one thing today that reflects God's
goodness to someone else.

Phase 2
Reflection

Strength Forged, Faith Refined

Take a steady breath.

You have walked through a refining season of your Holy Rise Up. This was not a phase meant to make you comfortable. It was meant to make you strong. The pressure you faced did not come to break you, but to shape your character and deepen your trust in God.

These weeks required endurance. You learned that real strength is not loud or rushed. It is steady. It is the discipline to keep showing up when the process feels slow and the outcome is still forming. You discovered that surrender is not weakness. It is the place where God's power is allowed to work fully.

You are not the same person who entered this phase. Your roots are deeper. Your convictions are clearer. Your faith is no longer based on emotion, but anchored in truth. You faced resistance and found resilience. You walked through testing and realized you are still standing, steadier than before.

This refining was never meant to last forever. It was preparation. Lift your head. What was tested has been strengthened. What was refined is now ready.

Journal Prompts

What trials or challenges in this phase strengthened my faith the most?

Where did I see God's hand shaping my character?

What habits, thoughts, or attitudes were refined out of me?

How has my definition of strength changed through this process?

Refined in Faith

Prayer

Lord, thank You for refining my heart, my habits, and my hope. You have removed what held me back and built a foundation that cannot be shaken.

Help me carry this endurance forward, not with pride, but with purpose.

May every challenge I face remind me that You are strengthening me and anchoring me deeper in truth.

Amen.

Affirmation

I am refined, resilient, and rooted in faith that cannot be moved.

Phase 3

Courage Under Fire

This is the phase where faith meets the flames.

You have been rooted in truth and refined in faith, and now it is time to rise with courage. This season will test what you believe, but it will also prove who you are. The fire does not come to destroy you; it comes to reveal the strength that God has already placed within you.

When life presses hard and pressure builds, remember this; courage is not the absence of fear, it is obedience in the face of it. Every test, every challenge, every unseen battle is a chance to show that your faith is unshakable.

You will stand taller in this phase, not because life gets easier, but because your trust gets stronger. The roar of your spirit will rise from the heat of resistance. And through it all, God will be the steady hand that turns your trials into triumphs.

So take heart. Lift your head high. The fire you face will become the forge that shapes your courage.

Day 131
Stand Strong in the Battle

May 11

"Be strong and courageous. Do not be afraid; do not be discouraged, for the Lord your God will be with you wherever you go."
Joshua 1:9

The battle is meant to build you, not break you. Every time you choose courage over comfort, heaven advances.

Affirmation: I am fearless because God stands beside me.

Rise Up Challenge: When doubt rises, declare aloud, "The Lord is with me. I will not fear."

Day 132
Faith Under Pressure

May 12

"We are hard pressed on every side, but not crushed;
perplexed, but not in despair."
2 Corinthians 4:8

Pressure exposes what's real. Let it press you closer to the presence of God, not further from it.

Affirmation: I stay steadfast under pressure; my faith will not fold.

Rise Up Challenge: When stress appears, pause and pray instead of reacting.

Day 133
The Fire That Forms You

May 13

"For our God is a consuming fire."
Hebrews 12:29

God never promised the absence of fire. He promised His presence within it, and the blaze refines the brave.

Affirmation: I walk through fire covered by divine protection.

Rise Up Challenge: Thank God today for one trial that made you stronger.

Day 134
Fearless Faith

May 14

"For God has not given us a spirit of fear, but of power, love, and a sound mind."
2 Timothy 1:7

Fear has no claim where faith stands firm. Courage is not the absence of fear, but the decision to move forward knowing Who is leading.

Affirmation: I walk in power, love, and peace; fear has no authority here.

Rise Up Challenge: Each time fear whispers, answer with this verse aloud.

Day 135
Armor Up

May 15

"Put on the full armor of God, so that you can take your stand against the devil's schemes."
Ephesians 6:11

Spiritual courage begins with spiritual armor. Truth, righteousness, and readiness guard the brave.

Affirmation: I am covered in God's armor; no attack can shake me.

Rise Up Challenge: Visualize putting on each piece of armor before you start your day.

Day 136
Courage to Speak

May 16

"Do not be afraid of them, for I am with you and will rescue you," declares the Lord.
Jeremiah 1:8

Boldness answers when God calls. Truth deserves a voice. Courage steps forward and speaks.

Affirmation: I speak with holy confidence, guided by God's truth.

Rise Up Challenge: Share one truth today that honors God's word, even if it is spoken quietly.

Day 137
The Lion's Heart

May 17

"The wicked flee though no one pursues, but the righteous are as bold as a lion."
Proverbs 28:1

Courage roars from righteousness. When your heart is right with God, boldness becomes your nature.

Affirmation: I carry the heart of a lion; righteousness fuels my roar.

Rise Up Challenge: Step into one task today with fearless confidence.

Day 138
Victory Through Obedience

May 18

"If you are willing and obedient, you will eat the good things of the land."
Isaiah 1:19

Obedience is the quiet courage that leads to victory. When you move at God's command, blessings follow.

Affirmation: My courage is shown through obedience.

Rise Up Challenge: Follow one prompting from God today without hesitation.

Day 139
When Faith Fights Fatigue

May 19

"So do not throw away your confidence; it will be richly rewarded."
Hebrews 10:35

I remain faithful when I am tired. God strengthens my endurance and renews my resolve. I stay committed until the harvest comes.

Affirmation: I don't quit. I endure with faith until fruit appears.

Rise Up Challenge: Recommit to something God asked you to keep doing.

Day 140
Courage in the Unknown

May 20

"Your word is a lamp for my feet, a light on my path."
Psalm 119:105

You don't need to see the whole road to walk it. Courage trusts the next step illuminated by His word.

Affirmation: I trust the light I have; God guides every step.

Rise Up Challenge: Move forward on one decision today, trusting His direction.

Day 141
Battle-Ready Peace

May 21

"The Lord will fight for you; you need only to be still."
Exodus 14:14

Courage doesn't always charge. It sometimes stands still in sacred confidence. Peace is a weapon when your trust is in Him.

Affirmation: I rest in divine peace while God fights for me.

Rise Up Challenge: Practice silence before reacting today; let God go first.

Day 142

When Faith Faces Fear

May 22

"The Lord is my helper; I will not be afraid.
What can mere mortals do to me?"
Hebrews 13:6

Courage isn't denying fear. It's walking through it with faith.
The shadow may surround you, but the Shepherd leads you
through.

Affirmation: I walk through darkness guided by God's light.

Rise Up Challenge: Confront one fear today, reminding yourself
you're never alone.

Day 143
Stand and See

May 23

"Do not be afraid. Stand firm and you will see the deliverance the Lord will bring you today."
Exodus 14:13

When the enemy advances, courage stands instead of scrambles. Stillness reveals salvation.

Affirmation: I stand firm and watch God move on my behalf.

Rise Up Challenge: Instead of reacting, respond with prayer and confidence today.

Day 144
Fireproof Faith

May 24

"In all this you greatly rejoice, though now for a little while you may have had to suffer grief in all kinds of trials. These have come so that the proven genuineness of your faith, of greater worth than gold, may result in praise, glory, and honor when Jesus Christ is revealed."
1 Peter 1:6–7

Trials reveal what time cannot tarnish. Faith that endures the fire is faith that has been refined. What remains after the heat is what is holy.

Affirmation: My faith is genuine, tested, and triumphant.

Rise Up Challenge: Write down one hardship and reflect on how it has strengthened your endurance.

Day 145
Strength to Stand

May 25

"Therefore put on the full armor of God, so that when the day of evil comes, you may be able to stand your ground."
Ephesians 6:13

Courage doesn't collapse under pressure; it holds the line. When others waver, you stay anchored in truth and fortified by faith.

Affirmation: I stand my ground, armored in truth and strength.

Rise Up Challenge: Declare aloud, "I am standing in the strength of God," before starting your day.

Day 146
The Power of Persistence

May 26

"Then Jesus told His disciples a parable to show them that they should always pray and not give up."
Luke 18:1

Persistence is courage in motion. Faith keeps praying when results delay. God hears every cry, even in silence.

Affirmation: I pray with endurance and wait with strength.

Rise Up Challenge: Revisit one prayer you've stopped praying and lift it again today.

Day 147
Courage to Confront

May 27

*"Fear not, for I am with you; be not
dismayed, for I am your God."*
Isaiah 41:10

True courage doesn't avoid conflict. It faces it with humility and
truth. God equips you to stand where others step back.

Affirmation: I face what must be faced with boldness and grace.

Rise Up Challenge: Address one challenge or conversation
you've been avoiding.

Day 148
The Fire Within

May 28

"His word is in my heart like a fire, a fire shut up in my bones; I am weary of holding it in; indeed, I cannot."
Jeremiah 20:9

The fire within you is the Spirit's power, not anger or pride. When you let that flame lead, it becomes light to others.

Affirmation: God's fire burns in me for His glory.

Rise Up Challenge: Share one encouragement today that ignites hope in someone else.

Day 149
Faith That Fights Back

May 29

*"Submit yourselves, then, to God. Resist the
devil, and he will flee from you."*
James 4:7

Faith doesn't run. It resists. The enemy can't overpower the
believer who stands submitted to God's authority.

Affirmation: I resist evil and stand strong under God's
command.

Rise Up Challenge: When temptation comes, speak this verse
out loud as your declaration.

Day 150
Courage in Surrender

May 30

"Not my will, but Yours be done."
Luke 22:42

Surrender is sacred strength. True warriors know victory comes from yielding control to the One who leads.

Affirmation: I surrender in strength, trusting God's will completely.

Rise Up Challenge: Hand over one thing you've been trying to control and trust Him with it today.

Day 151
Faith That Defends

May 31

"Always be prepared to give an answer to everyone who asks you to give the reason for the hope that you have."
1 Peter 3:15

Defending your faith isn't about debate. It's about devotion. Speak truth with love, and courage will carry your words.

Affirmation: My courage defends the hope within me.

Rise Up Challenge: Share your testimony briefly with someone who needs encouragement.

Day 152
Unbreakable Focus

June 1

*"Fixing our eyes on Jesus, the pioneer and
perfecter of faith."*
Hebrews 12:2

Focus fuels courage. When your eyes stay fixed on Christ,
distractions lose their power.

Affirmation: My gaze is steady on Jesus; my courage stays
clear.

Rise Up Challenge: Limit one distraction today that competes
with your focus on God.

Day 153
Standing in the Gap

June 2

"I looked for someone among them who would build up the wall and stand before Me in the gap on behalf of the land."
Ezekiel 22:30

Courage stands in intercession when others stand aside. God uses those willing to pray for what others overlook.

Affirmation: I stand in the gap through prayer, strength, and purpose.

Rise Up Challenge: Pray intentionally for someone who can't pray for themselves today.

Day 154
The Courage to Forgive

June 3

"Bear with each other and forgive one another if any of you has a grievance against someone. Forgive as the Lord forgave you."
Colossians 3:13

Forgiveness is fierce courage. It frees your heart to fight with love instead of bitterness.

Affirmation: I release offense and rise in peace.

Rise Up Challenge: Forgive one person silently in prayer and bless them as you do.

Day 155
Strength in Suffering

June 4

"But He said to me, 'My grace is sufficient for you,
for My power is made perfect in weakness.'"
2 Corinthians 12:9

Even pain has purpose when grace holds you. Courage shines brightest when strength is gone but faith remains.

Affirmation: God's grace sustains me through suffering.

Rise Up Challenge: When you feel weak, thank God aloud for His strength within you.

Day 156
Courage to Lead

June 5

"The greatest among you will be your servant."
Matthew 23:11

Leadership in God's kingdom begins with humility. Courage leads not for recognition but for righteousness.

Affirmation: I lead with humility and courage that honors God.

Rise Up Challenge: Serve quietly today where no one can see but God.

Day 157
Faith in the Waiting

June 6

"Those who hope in the Lord will renew their strength. They will soar on wings like eagles."
Isaiah 40:31

Waiting builds warriors. God renews strength not in the rush, but in the still moments of trust.

Affirmation: My hope soars higher than my waiting.

Rise Up Challenge: When impatience hits, pray this verse as your anchor.

Day 158
Battle-Tested Faith

June 7

*"Praise be to the Lord my Rock, who trains my hands
for war, my fingers for battle."*
Psalm 144:1

Every challenge is training ground. The warrior of faith learns
endurance through every trial.

Affirmation: I am battle-tested and Spirit-trained.

Rise Up Challenge: Reflect on one hardship that strengthened
your spiritual skill.

Day 159
Courage to Continue

June 8

*"I press on toward the goal to win the prize for which
God has called me heavenward in Christ Jesus."*
Philippians 3:14

Courage doesn't always roar. It keeps moving forward.
Perseverance is holy momentum.

Affirmation: I press on, no matter what stands ahead.

Rise Up Challenge: Take one step today toward a long-term
goal you've paused.

Day 160
The Fire of Faithfulness

June 9

"His master replied, 'Well done, good and faithful servant! You have been faithful with a few things; I will put you in charge of many things. Come and share your master's happiness!'"
Matthew 25:21

Faithfulness under fire reveals true courage. When you're steady with the small, God trusts you with the greater.

Affirmation: My courage is proven through daily faithfulness.

Rise Up Challenge: Be intentionally excellent in one small task today.

Day 161
Strength in the Storm

June 10

"The Lord is my refuge and my fortress, my God, in whom I trust."
Psalm 91:2

When storms rise, courage stays anchored. The winds may howl, but your shelter is unshakable because your faith is built on the Rock.

Affirmation: My refuge is in God; no storm can move me.

Rise Up Challenge: Each time anxiety hits today, whisper, "You are my fortress, Lord."

Day 162
Courage That Perseveres

June 11

"Consider it pure joy, my brothers and sisters, whenever you face trials of many kinds, because you know that the testing of your faith produces perseverance."
James 1:2-3

Joy in trials is discipline. Testing trains the warrior. Perseverance proves maturity.

Affirmation: Every test is producing strength within me.

Rise Up Challenge: Reframe one challenge today as spiritual training.

Day 163
Faith That Doesn't Flinch

June 12

"I have set the Lord always before me. Because He is at my right hand, I will not be shaken."
Psalm 16:8

When faith fixes its gaze on God, fear loses its grip. Courage is calm because confidence comes from His nearness.

Affirmation: I stand unshaken with God beside me.

Rise Up Challenge: When faced with uncertainty, pause and visualize His presence at your right hand.

Day 164
The Strength of Steadfast Faith

June 13

"Be on your guard; stand firm in the faith; be courageous; be strong."
1 Corinthians 16:13

Steadfastness is a daily decision. Courage shows up not once but every morning you rise to face the day's battles.

Affirmation: I choose strength again today, faithful, focused, and fearless.

Rise Up Challenge: Start your day declaring this verse as your foundation.

Day 165
Victory in the Valley

June 14

"Even though I walk through the valley of the shadow of death, I will fear no evil, for You are with me."
Psalm 23:4

Victory isn't only found on mountaintops. God trains courage in valleys where shadows fall and trust is tested.

Affirmation: I walk through valleys with victory in my spirit.

Rise Up Challenge: Reflect on a low season and thank God for how He walked you through.

Day 166
Courage That Endures

June 15

"Blessed is the one who perseveres under trial because, having stood the test, that person will receive the crown of life that the Lord has promised to those who love Him."
James 1:12

Endurance is courage stretched over time. The crown belongs to those who keep standing when it would be easier to quit.

Affirmation: My endurance is my worship; I won't give up.

Rise Up Challenge: Commit to finishing something today you've been tempted to abandon.

Day 167
Faith That Roars

June 16

"The righteous cry out, and the Lord hears them; He delivers them from all their troubles."
Psalm 34:17

A lion's courage is found in prayer that rises through pain. Heaven moves when faith finds its voice.

Affirmation: My cry is my courage; God hears me when I roar.

Rise Up Challenge: Pray boldly out loud today for one need in your life.

Day 168
Strength in the Struggle

June 17

"My flesh and my heart may fail, but God is the strength of my heart and my portion forever."
Psalm 73:26

The struggle does not signal defeat. It reveals dependence. True courage admits weakness and keeps moving forward.

Affirmation: God's strength fills my weakness.

Rise Up Challenge: When frustration rises, breathe deeply and say, "You are my strength, Lord."

Day 169
Courage That Endures the Fire

June 18

"The Lord is faithful, and He will strengthen you and protect you from the evil one."
2 Thessalonians 3:3

Even in the heat, God's faithfulness never falters. His protection does not remove the fire but preserves you through it.

Affirmation: I am strengthened and guarded by God's faithfulness.

Rise Up Challenge: Thank Him for unseen protection over your life today.

Day 170
Faith That Commands Peace

June 19

"He got up, rebuked the wind and said to the waves, 'Quiet! Be still!' Then the wind died down and it was completely calm."
Mark 4:39

Courage does not panic. It speaks peace into chaos. The same power that calmed the storm in Galilee lives within you.

Affirmation: I carry the authority of peace wherever I go.

Rise Up Challenge: When tension rises, speak calm words instead of reacting.

Day 171
Strength to Rebuild

June 20

"The God of heaven will give us success. We His servants will start rebuilding."
Nehemiah 2:20

Courage does not just survive. It rebuilds. When God calls you to restore what was broken, He supplies the strength to finish.

Affirmation: I rebuild with God's power and purpose.

Rise Up Challenge: Take one small step today toward rebuilding something that once fell apart.

Day 172

Courage That Overcomes

June 21

*"Do not be overcome by evil, but
overcome evil with good."*
Romans 12:21

Evil loses power when goodness takes the lead. The greatest
battles are won not by revenge, but by righteousness.

Affirmation: I overcome evil with divine goodness and grace.

Rise Up Challenge: Respond to one negative action today with
intentional kindness.

Day 173
Strength in the Waiting

June 22

"The Lord is good to those whose hope is in Him, to the one who seeks Him."
Lamentations 3:25

Waiting is not wasted. It is where faith matures. God is still working while you are still waiting.

Affirmation: My waiting is not empty. It's filled with faith.

Rise Up Challenge: Write down what you're waiting for and one way you'll trust God through it.

Day 174
Courage That Conquers Fear

June 23

"I sought the Lord, and He answered me; He delivered me from all my fears."
Psalm 34:4

Fear does not vanish by force. It is conquered by pursuit. The moment you seek God, fear loses its voice.

Affirmation: God delivers me from fear; I rise with courage and calm.

Rise Up Challenge: When fear visits today, pray immediately and thank God for deliverance.

Phase 3
Reflection
Courage Under Fire

Take a deep breath, warrior of faith.

You've stood in the flames and come out refined. This phase was never about avoiding heat; it was about discovering what you're made of when the temperature rises.

You've learned that courage isn't loud. It's loyal. It shows up in quiet trust, steady endurance, and faith that refuses to back down. Every trial trained your spirit, every fire forged your focus, and every storm revealed strength that cannot be shaken.

You've faced what tried to break you and found that God was building you. Now, you stand bolder, wiser, and more grounded in truth than ever before.

Where did I choose obedience over comfort during this phase?

Which trial or pressure strengthened my faith the most?

How has my understanding of courage changed through this season?

What strength has been forged in me that I can carry into the next phase?

Prayer

Lord, thank You for walking with me through the fire.

You were present in every test and faithful when my strength felt thin. You did not remove the flames, but You strengthened me within them.

Teach me to carry this courage forward as faith that trusts You completely. When future trials come, remind me that I have already stood and already endured.

I place my confidence not in myself, but in You, the God who refines, protects, and strengthens me through every season.
Amen.

Affirmation

I am courageous, steadfast, and strengthened by God. The fire did not consume me. It strengthened me.

Phase 4

Stand in Purpose

The time of testing has produced clarity. Now you rise, not just to survive, but to stand.

Phase 4 is where courage turns into conviction. It's about walking in purpose with confidence, owning the mission God has entrusted to you, and standing tall in character when compromise calls your name.

In this next phase, you'll learn what it means to live with vision, discipline, and divine direction. Every step will be guided by purpose, every word anchored in truth, and every action aimed toward Kingdom impact.

The fires of refinement are behind you. Now you walk forward as a man of purpose, rooted, ready, and resolved.

Day 175
Walking in Purpose

June 24

"The Lord makes firm the steps of the one who delights in Him; though he may stumble, he will not fall, for the Lord upholds him with His hand."
Psalm 37:23-24

Purpose is not a path you discover once. It is one you choose daily. God orders every step, even the ones that feel uncertain. When you walk in His will, every stumble becomes a setup for strength.

Affirmation: My steps are directed by God, and every stride carries purpose.

Rise Up Challenge: Take one intentional step today toward a calling you've delayed. Trust that God steadies each move.

Day 176
Built for the Battle

June 25

"Finally, be strong in the Lord and in His mighty power. Put on the full armor of God so that you can take your stand against the devil's schemes."
Ephesians 6:10-11

Standing in purpose means knowing you are built for the battle. Armor up, not in pride, but in preparation. Each morning you choose faith over fear, you are already gaining ground.

Affirmation: I wear God's armor with confidence and conviction.

Rise Up Challenge: Before your day begins, pray through each piece of the armor of God and picture yourself equipped for victory.

Day 177
The Power of Conviction

June 26

"Stand firm then, with the belt of truth buckled around your waist."
Ephesians 6:14

Conviction guards your character when compromise tempts you. Truth anchors you. Standing firm begins within.

Affirmation: I am anchored in truth and unwavering in conviction.

Rise Up Challenge: Identify one area of your life where truth must lead, even if it costs you comfort.

Day 178
Purpose Over Pride

June 27

"Humble yourselves, therefore, under God's mighty hand, that He may lift you up in due time."
1 Peter 5:6

Purpose is shaped by humility. Strength is revealed through surrender and lived out in service that honors God.

Affirmation: My purpose thrives in humility. God's strength shines through my surrender.

Rise Up Challenge: Do one humble act today that gives glory to God, not to yourself.

Day 179
Standing Strong in Character

June 28

"The integrity of the upright guides them, but the unfaithful are destroyed by their duplicity."
Proverbs 11:3

Character is the unseen strength behind every victory. Standing in purpose means choosing integrity when no one is watching. God builds greatness on the foundation of honesty.

Affirmation: My integrity is my armor; my actions reflect my faith.

Rise Up Challenge: Make one decision today that honors truth, even if no one notices.

Day 180
Standing Battle-Ready

June 29

"Put on the full armor of God, so that you can take your stand against the devil's schemes."
Ephesians 6:11

Purpose is not passive; it is preparation. Every trial has trained you for this moment. When you stand clothed in truth, righteousness, and faith, you are already equipped for victory.

Affirmation: I am armed with faith and ready for every battle God leads me through.

Rise Up Challenge: Pray Ephesians 6:10–18 out loud as your armor prayer today.

Day 181
Purpose That Perseveres

June 30

"Blessed is the one who perseveres under trial because, having stood the test, that person will receive the crown of life."
James 1:12

Your purpose will be tested, but perseverance produces purity. When you keep showing up with faith, God crowns your endurance with honor.

Affirmation: My perseverance is power. Every trial refines my strength.

Rise Up Challenge: Reflect on one past challenge and how it shaped your resilience.

Day 182
Stand Tall in Truth

July 1

"Sanctify them by the truth; Your word is truth."
John 17:17

Truth is your foundation. When the world twists, truth keeps you upright. Standing tall in God's Word keeps you unshaken when lies surround you.

Affirmation: I am grounded in truth and unmoved by falsehood.

Rise Up Challenge: Speak one Scripture aloud that reinforces your faith today.

Day 183
Purpose Over Popularity

July 2

"For what does it profit a man to gain the whole world, yet forfeit his soul?"
Mark 8:36

Standing in purpose often means standing alone. Don't trade your integrity for acceptance. God's approval outweighs every earthly applause.

Affirmation: I choose purpose over popularity. My value is rooted in Christ, not opinion.

Rise Up Challenge: Take one action today that aligns with conviction, not convenience.

Day 184
Strength in Obedience

July 3

"If you love Me, keep My commands."
John 14:15

Obedience is not about control. It is about connection. Every act of obedience strengthens your faith and builds spiritual muscle for the journey ahead.

Affirmation: My obedience builds strength and deepens my faith.

Rise Up Challenge: Follow one nudge from the Holy Spirit today without hesitation.

Day 185
Unshaken Purpose

July 4

*"Those who trust in the Lord are like Mount Zion,
which cannot be shaken but endures forever."*
Psalm 125:1

God's purpose in you is unshakable because it's built on His eternal foundation. When life trembles, stand firm. The ground beneath you is holy.

Affirmation: I am rooted and unshaken, standing strong in divine purpose.

Rise Up Challenge: Declare today, "Nothing can move me from God's plan for my life."

Day 186
Led by the Spirit

July 5

"For those who are led by the Spirit of God are the children of God."
Romans 8:14

To stand in purpose means to move with divine direction. The Spirit leads where your own understanding cannot. Let Him guide your every step today.

Affirmation: I follow the Spirit's lead and walk confidently in divine direction.

Rise Up Challenge: Spend five minutes asking the Holy Spirit to lead your decisions today.

Day 187
Courage to Keep Going

July 6

"Wait for the Lord; be strong and take heart and wait for the Lord."
Psalm 27:14

Purpose demands courage. You are not called to comfort but to boldness. Every step you take in faith reveals a God who walks beside you.

Affirmation: I rise with courage. God's strength fuels every step I take.

Rise Up Challenge: Do one thing today that scares you but aligns with your purpose.

Day 188
Purpose in the Waiting

July 7

"The Lord is good to those whose hope is in Him, to the one who seeks Him."
Lamentations 3:25

Waiting is not wasted when you wait with faith. The pause prepares you. God builds strength, wisdom, and perspective in the still seasons.

Affirmation: I wait with purpose. God is working even in my stillness.

Rise Up Challenge: Use today to rest in faith instead of striving for results.

Day 189
Steadfast Focus

July 8

"Let your eyes look straight ahead; fix your gaze directly before you."
Proverbs 4:25

Purpose requires focus. When distractions rise, determination must lead. Keep your eyes on the mission, not the noise.

Affirmation: My focus is firm. I fix my eyes on God's purpose and refuse distraction.

Rise Up Challenge: Remove one distraction that pulls you away from your goals today.

Day 190

Strength in Surrender

July 9

"Submit yourselves therefore to God. Resist the devil, and he will flee from you."
James 4:7

True strength is found in surrender. When you stop fighting for control, God lifts you higher than your striving ever could.

Affirmation: My surrender is my strength. God's timing will always lift me.

Rise Up Challenge: Pray over one area of life you are still trying to control, and let it go.

Day 191
Stand Bold in Conviction

July 10

*"Watch, stand fast in the faith,
be brave, be strong."*
1 Corinthians 16:13

Conviction is courage anchored in truth. When others compromise, you hold your ground. Standing bold means choosing faith even when it costs comfort.

Affirmation: I stand firm in my convictions and walk in unshakable faith.

Rise Up Challenge: Speak one truth today, even if your voice trembles.

Day 192
Purpose in the Process

July 11

"For we walk by faith, not by sight."
2 Corinthians 5:7

Purpose is a journey of trust. Even when the path looks unclear, God's direction is steady. Faith fills the gaps where clarity is missing.

Affirmation: I trust the process because I trust the One guiding it.

Rise Up Challenge: Write one area where you will choose faith over control today.

Day 193
Power in Perseverance

July 12

"You need to persevere so that when you have done the will of God, you will receive what He has promised."
Hebrews 10:36

Purpose thrives through perseverance. Every challenge you endure refines the strength of your faith and builds spiritual stamina.

Affirmation: My perseverance paves the path to God's promises.

Rise Up Challenge: Reflect on one past victory that came through perseverance.

Day 194
Faith That Stands Firm

July 13

"Therefore, my dear brothers and sisters, stand firm. Let nothing move you."
1 Corinthians 15:58

Faith that stands firm is not loud; it is loyal. It stays planted even when progress feels invisible. Stability is strength disguised as stillness.

Affirmation: My faith stands firm, unshaken by delay or doubt.

Rise Up Challenge: When impatience rises, whisper, "I will not be moved."

Day 195
Grounded in Gratitude

July 14

"Give thanks in all circumstances; for this is God's will for you in Christ Jesus."
1 Thessalonians 5:18

Gratitude grounds your purpose in peace. When you thank God in everything, even hardship becomes holy. Gratitude keeps your spirit from drifting.

Affirmation: Gratitude steadies my heart and strengthens my faith.

Rise Up Challenge: Write three things you are thankful for that once felt like struggles.

Day 196
Unyielding Purpose

July 15

*"I press on toward the goal to win the prize for which
God has called me heavenward in Christ Jesus."*
Philippians 3:14

Standing in purpose requires persistence. Keep pressing forward.
What you are building in faith will outlast fatigue.

Affirmation: I press forward with perseverance and passion.

Rise Up Challenge: Take one small step toward your calling
today, no matter how minor it feels.

Day 197
Strength Through Suffering

July 16

*"After you have suffered a little while, God will restore
you and make you strong, firm, and steadfast."*
1 Peter 5:10

Suffering is not the end of your story. It is strength in disguise.
God uses hardship to anchor your purpose in endurance.

Affirmation: I grow stronger through every season of struggle.

Rise Up Challenge: Reflect on one hardship that deepened your
compassion or faith.

Day 198
Anchored in Faith

July 17

*"Trust in the Lord with all your heart and lean not
on your own understanding."*
Proverbs 3:5–6

Faith anchors your purpose when feelings waver. Even when the
future looks uncertain, faith steadies your direction.

Affirmation: My faith anchors my steps and my purpose
remains firm.

Rise Up Challenge: Replace one worry with a prayer of trust
today.

Day 199
The Courage to Rise Again

July 18

*"For though the righteous fall seven times,
they rise again."*
Proverbs 24:16

Failure is not final when your faith remains alive. Courage
means standing up one more time than you fall. Rising is part of
your refining.

Affirmation: I rise again with courage, grace, and renewed
strength.

Rise Up Challenge: Reflect on one time you got back up
stronger than before.

Day 200
Purpose in Peace

July 19

"You will keep in perfect peace those whose minds are steadfast, because they trust in You."
Isaiah 26:3

Peace is not the absence of pressure but the presence of purpose. When your mission aligns with God's will, peace becomes your strength.

Affirmation: My peace fuels my purpose and keeps me strong.

Rise Up Challenge: Choose peace in one situation that usually stirs frustration.

Day 201
Rooted in Obedience

July 20

"Blessed are all who fear the Lord, who walk in obedience to Him."
Psalm 128:1

Obedience roots your purpose in blessing. It is not about perfection but posture. God rewards the heart that listens and follows with faith.

Affirmation: I am rooted in obedience and grounded in faith.

Rise Up Challenge: Ask God for guidance before making one decision today.

Day 202
Strength That Stands

July 21

"He gives strength to the weary and increases the power of the weak."
Isaiah 40:29

Even warriors need renewal. God's strength never runs out; it replenishes you exactly when you need it most.

Affirmation: My strength comes from God and never runs dry.

Rise Up Challenge: Pause for five minutes and breathe deeply, thanking God for His sustaining power.

Day 203
Steadfast in Mission

July 22

"Let us not become weary in doing good, for at the proper time we will reap a harvest if we do not give up."
Galatians 6:9

Mission requires stamina. Purpose is not fulfilled overnight; it grows through consistency. Every small act of faith contributes to the bigger picture.

Affirmation: I remain steadfast in my mission, trusting God with the results.

Rise Up Challenge: Do one good deed today without expecting recognition.

Day 204
The Power of
Perspective

July 23

"For our light and momentary troubles are achieving for us an eternal glory that far outweighs them all."
2 Corinthians 4:17

Perspective shifts the way you see pressure. Trials become training when viewed through God's eternal lens.

Affirmation: I see every challenge as preparation for purpose.

Rise Up Challenge: When frustration arises, say, "This is forming me, not defeating me."

Day 205
Firm in Faith

July 24

"Resist him, standing firm in the faith, because you know that the family of believers throughout the world is undergoing the same kind of sufferings."
1 Peter 5:9

Standing firm means knowing you are not alone. The same God who holds others upright will hold you steady too.

Affirmation: I stand firm in faith and find strength in unity.

Rise Up Challenge: Pray for someone else who is walking through a trial.

Day 206
Confidence in Calling

July 25

"The one who calls you is faithful, and He will do it."
1 Thessalonians 5:24

Confidence is not arrogance; it is assurance in the One who called you. God finishes what He starts, and you are part of His masterpiece.

Affirmation: My confidence is rooted in God's faithfulness, not my own ability.

Rise Up Challenge: Write one declaration that reminds you of your divine calling.

Day 207
Peaceful Presence

July 26

"Be still, and know that I am God."
Psalm 46:10

Restoration deepens your presence. You no longer rush or reach; you rest. God's power moves through a quiet heart that listens more than it speaks. Peace is found in awareness, not escape.

Affirmation: I move through life with calm strength. My presence reflects God's peace.

Rise Up Challenge: Spend five minutes today in silence. Breathe slowly and let God's peace meet you there.

Day 208
Strength in Still Seasons

July 27

"The Lord will fight for you; you need only to be still."
Exodus 14:14

Even when life slows down, God is still working. Waiting is not weakness. It is strength under discipline. Still seasons shape endurance, not apathy.

Affirmation: My stillness is power. I trust God to move even when I stand still.

Rise Up Challenge: Resist the urge to force progress. Choose one thing to leave in God's hands today.

Day 209
The Power of Gratitude

July 28

"Give thanks to the Lord, for He is good; His love endures forever."
Psalm 107:1

Gratitude turns battle scars into badges of honor. When you thank God in every season, you transform trials into testimonies. Gratitude does not ignore pain; it declares victory in the middle of it.

Affirmation: Gratitude keeps my heart strong and my faith focused.

Rise Up Challenge: Write three things you are grateful for right now, even if they stretched you to grow.

Day 210
Anchored in Peace

July 29

*"We have this hope as an anchor for the soul, firm
and secure."*
Hebrews 6:19

True power is quiet confidence. Peace isn't the absence of battle
but the certainty of victory. When you walk with purpose, peace
becomes your anchor in every storm.

Affirmation: My peace is anchored in God's promises. My
purpose stands firm.

Rise Up Challenge: When tension rises today, choose peace
over pressure. Let calm lead the way.

Day 211
Strength in the Struggle

July 30

"I can do all things through Christ who strengthens me."
Philippians 4:13

Strength isn't proven by what you lift, but by what you carry with grace. Even when you feel stretched thin, God is strengthening your spirit for the climb ahead.

Affirmation: My strength comes from Christ within me. I rise through every challenge.

Rise Up Challenge: Do one thing today that requires perseverance, not perfection.

Day 212
Strength in Simplicity

July 31

"What does the Lord require of you? To act justly, love mercy, and walk humbly with your God."
Micah 6:8

The foundation of purpose is simple: justice, mercy, and humility. You do not need to strive for greatness when God has already defined what matters.

Affirmation: My life reflects simplicity, mercy, and humility before God.

Rise Up Challenge: Simplify one part of your day and fill it with gratitude instead.

Day 213
Stand in Confidence

August 1

"So do not throw away your confidence; it will be richly rewarded."
Hebrews 10:35

Confidence in Christ keeps you steady when challenges come. Your assurance is not arrogance; it is faith anchored in truth.

Affirmation: I walk in quiet confidence, knowing God rewards bold faith.

Rise Up Challenge: Speak one confident declaration of faith over your life today.

Day 214
Purpose That Prevails

August 2

"Many are the plans in a person's heart, but it is the Lord's purpose that prevails."
Proverbs 19:21

Purpose outlasts plans. When life doesn't go your way, remember that God's design still stands. His purpose never fails, even when yours shifts.

Affirmation: God's purpose prevails in every part of my story.

Rise Up Challenge: Release one plan to God today and trust Him to redirect it perfectly.

Day 215
Strength That Endures

August 3

"But the one who stands firm to the end will be saved."
Matthew 24:13

Endurance isn't glamorous, but it is sacred. Strength that endures is built through consistency and trust. God honors those who stay steady when others give up.

Affirmation: My endurance honors God. I stand firm to the end.

Rise Up Challenge: Finish one task today that you have been putting off, as an act of faithfulness.

Day 216
Purpose That Protects

August 4

"The Lord will keep you from all harm; He will watch over your life."
Psalm 121:7

When you walk in purpose, God's protection surrounds you. You are covered not because of perfection, but because you are walking in divine direction.

Affirmation: I am protected in my purpose. God watches over every step I take.

Rise Up Challenge: Pray Psalm 121 over yourself or your family today.

Day 217
Strength in Brotherhood

August 5

"As iron sharpens iron, so one person sharpens another."
Proverbs 27:17

God never designed you to stand alone. Brotherhood refines courage, accountability, and truth. Strength grows stronger when it's shared.

Affirmation: I grow stronger through godly brotherhood and accountability.

Rise Up Challenge: Reach out to a friend or brother in faith and encourage them today.

Day 218
Rooted in Wisdom

August 6

*"The fear of the Lord is the beginning of wisdom,
and knowledge of the Holy One is understanding."*
Proverbs 9:10

Purpose without wisdom wavers. Wisdom roots you in discernment and keeps you aligned when emotions rise. Seek understanding more than applause.

Affirmation: I am rooted in wisdom and guided by understanding.

Rise Up Challenge: Read one chapter of Proverbs today and reflect on its wisdom.

Day 219
Purpose That Builds Others

August 7

*"Therefore encourage one another and
build each other up."*
1 Thessalonians 5:11

Your purpose is never just about you. It is about the lives your
faith touches. Every word of encouragement you speak builds
something eternal.

Affirmation: My purpose uplifts others and reflects God's
love.

Rise Up Challenge: Encourage someone who might be
struggling in silence today.

Day 220
Strength in Submission

August 8

"Humble yourselves before the Lord, and He will lift you up."
James 4:10

Submission is surrender to divine authority. A true warrior yields to God first, trusting that obedience shapes lasting strength.

Affirmation: I find my strength in surrendering to God's authority.

Rise Up Challenge: Surrender one decision to God today instead of rushing your own way.

Day 221
Purpose That Perseveres

August 9

*"Let perseverance finish its work so that you may
be mature and complete, not lacking anything."*
James 1:4

Purpose matures through patience. The more you allow God to
refine you, the stronger your foundation becomes. Perseverance
shapes your power.

Affirmation: I am being perfected through perseverance and
patience.

Rise Up Challenge: Reflect on how your current challenges
might be refining your character.

Day 222
Anchored by Grace

August 10

"My grace is sufficient for you, for My power is made perfect in weakness."
2 Corinthians 12:9

Grace anchors you when strength runs out. God's power shines brightest when you stop striving and start surrendering.

Affirmation: Grace sustains me. My weakness becomes God's strength.

Rise Up Challenge: Replace one self-critical thought today with a declaration of grace.

Day 223
Purpose That Prevails Through Pressure

August 11

"No, in all these things we are more than conquerors through Him who loved us."
Romans 8:37

Pressure purifies purpose. It doesn't destroy what's divine. It strengthens it. When life squeezes you, let faith be what flows out.

Affirmation: I prevail through pressure because God's power lives in me.

Rise Up Challenge: Respond to one stressful moment today with faith instead of frustration.

Day 224
Strength That Submits

August 12

"Be still before the Lord and wait patiently for Him."
Psalm 37:7

Patience is power under control. Strength that submits learns to trust. Waiting on God's timing is divine training.

Affirmation: My strength is disciplined by patience and grounded in trust.

Rise Up Challenge: Spend five minutes in quiet waiting before starting your day.

Day 225
Purpose Through Purity

August 13

"Blessed are the pure in heart, for they will see God."
Matthew 5:8

Purity keeps purpose clear. When your motives are aligned with God's will, your vision sharpens and your spirit stays strong.

Affirmation: My heart is pure, and my purpose remains clear before God.

Rise Up Challenge: Ask God to reveal any motive that needs refining today.

Day 226
Strength in Renewal

August 14

"He gives strength to the weary and increases the power of the weak."
Isaiah 40:29

Renewal is strength restored through surrender. You were never meant to run on empty. Hope in the Lord and He will lift you higher.

Affirmation: My strength is renewed daily by hope in the Lord.

Rise Up Challenge: Take ten deep breaths and whisper, "I am renewed in His strength."

Day 227
Purpose That Glorifies God

August 15

"So whether you eat or drink or whatever you do,
do it all for the glory of God."
1 Corinthians 10:31

Purpose without glory to God becomes performance. Every action is worship when done for His name. Live to glorify, not to impress.

Affirmation: My purpose glorifies God in every word and action.

Rise Up Challenge: Before one task today, pray, "Let this bring You glory, Lord."

Day 228
Courage to Stay Consistent

August 14

*""Let us run with perseverance the race marked
out for us."*
Hebrews 12:1

Consistency is courage in motion. Even when results seem slow, faithfulness keeps your fire burning. Keep showing up, because God's promise still stands.

Affirmation: I remain consistent because God remains faithful.

Rise Up Challenge: Stay committed to one daily discipline that strengthens your spirit.

Day 229
Strength in Restoration

August 17

*"He heals the brokenhearted and binds up their
wounds."*
Psalm 147:3

Restoration requires vulnerability. God restores what you
surrender. His presence revives what pain tried to bury.

Affirmation: I am restored through God's presence and peace.

Rise Up Challenge: Reflect on one area of your life where you
feel God's quiet restoration at work.

Day 230
Purpose That
Perseveres in Faith

August 18

"For we live by faith, not by sight."
2 Corinthians 5:7

Faith keeps your purpose alive when you cannot see progress. Trusting what you cannot yet see builds strength you cannot yet measure.

Affirmation: My faith fuels my purpose beyond what I can see.

Rise Up Challenge: Write one line of faith today: "I will believe until I see."

Day 231
Strength in Still Moments

August 19

"Be still, and know that I am God."
Psalm 46:10

Stillness is spiritual discipline. Strength forms beneath the surface when you slow down before God. In quiet moments, He restores your focus and strengthens your purpose.

Affirmation: My stillness is sacred. God works even when I rest.

Rise Up Challenge: Sit in silence for five minutes and thank God for His presence.

Day 232
Anchored in Hope

August 20

*"May the God of hope fill you with all joy and
peace as you trust in Him."*
Romans 15:13

Hope keeps purpose alive. When faith feels tired, hope keeps
you standing. It reminds you that God's faithfulness has never
failed.

Affirmation: I am anchored in hope and confident in God's
promises.

Rise Up Challenge: Write one area where you will hold fast to
hope this week.

Day 233
Purpose That Impacts Generations

August 21

"Teach them to your children and to their children after them."
Deuteronomy 4:9

Purpose becomes legacy when you pass it on. Your faith, your resilience, your courage are seeds that will outlive you.

Affirmation: My faith and purpose create a legacy that will endure.

Rise Up Challenge: Speak one life-giving truth over the next generation today.

Day 234
Strength That Finishes Well

August 22

"I have fought the good fight, I have finished the race, I have kept the faith."
2 Timothy 4:7

Finishing strong is not about speed but endurance. When you stand in purpose to the end, you reflect the strength of the One who carried you through.

Affirmation: I finish strong in faith and purpose, knowing God sustained me.

Rise Up Challenge: Reflect on how far you have come and thank God for His steady strength.

Phase 4
Reflection
Stand in Purpose

Take a deep breath and look back at the ground you have covered.

This was the phase where faith took action. Purpose stopped being a dream and became a direction. You have learned that strength is not proven by noise but by endurance. You have discovered that the roar of a lion often begins in quiet obedience.

You stood tall when it would have been easier to step back. You stayed grounded when the wind pressed hard against you. And through it all, you learned that purpose is not about perfection; it is about persistence.

This phase was about building muscle in your mission. Every act of faith, every prayer in the dark, every choice to stand when no one saw it, built the kind of character that Heaven can trust with victory.

You are not the same man who started this phase. You are standing stronger, clearer, and more confident in who you are and Who sent you.

Journal Prompts

What moments in this phase strengthened my conviction or courage?

How has obedience refined my purpose?

Where did I notice God's protection or direction most clearly?

What part of my character grew the most during this phase?

Stand in Purpose

Prayer

Lord, thank You for teaching me how to stand strong in Your purpose.

You have refined me, focused me, and filled me with conviction.

Help me to keep my eyes fixed on You, to move only by Your Spirit, and to use my strength to serve others.

Let my purpose reflect Your power and my life display Your glory.

Amen.

Affirmation

I am standing firm in my divine purpose. My strength is steady, my steps are guided, and my spirit is anchored in truth.

Phase 5

Rise in Victory

This is it, the phase of triumph, renewal, and revelation.

Every battle, every prayer, every ounce of perseverance has led to this moment. You are no longer just standing in purpose; you are rising in victory. This final phase is not about striving for strength; it is about walking in it. It is about recognizing that the victory is already won through Christ and that your part is to rise and live like it.

Victory does not always look like noise and crowns. Sometimes it looks like peace after pain, wisdom after warfare, and calm confidence after chaos. God has prepared you for this season of holy victory, one marked by praise.

So rise. Rise with courage. Rise with confidence. Rise with gratitude.

The roar of your faith will echo through every corner of your life and beyond.

Day 235
Rise Restored

August 23

*"He restores my soul; He guides me along the right
paths for His name's sake."*
Psalm 23:3

Restoration is renewal. God rebuilds what was worn and
strengthens what was tested. He shapes you through every battle
and prepares you for what lies ahead.

Affirmation: My soul is restored, and my steps are guided by
God's grace.

Rise Up Challenge: Reflect on one area of your life that God
has restored, and thank Him for the transformation.

Day 236
Victory Through Obedience

August 24

"If you are willing and obedient, you will eat the good things of the land."
Isaiah 1:19

Victory is not always found in striving but in surrender. Obedience opens doors that effort never could. When you walk in alignment, blessings follow naturally.

Affirmation: My obedience paves the way for victory.

Rise Up Challenge: Obey one small prompting from God today without delay.

Day 237
Strength in Stillness

August 25

"The Lord will fight for you; you need only to be still."
Exodus 14:14

Stillness is not weakness. It is a declaration of faith that God is in control. When you stop striving, He starts moving in ways unseen.

Affirmation: I find strength in stillness and peace in surrender.

Rise Up Challenge: Take five minutes of silence to rest in God's presence and release your worries.

Day 238
Rise Above Fear

August 26

"The Lord is my light and my salvation; whom shall I fear?"
Psalm 27:1

Fear loses its grip when faith takes the lead. Courage is not the absence of fear but the decision to trust God despite it.

Affirmation: My trust in God is greater than my fear.

Rise Up Challenge: When fear arises, pause and speak faith out loud.

Day 239
The Power of Praise

August 27

"I will bless the Lord at all times; His praise
will always be on my lips."
Psalm 34:1

Praise is a weapon. It shifts your focus from problems to power, from chaos to confidence. Victory begins with a grateful heart that glorifies God in all things.

Affirmation: My praise is powerful. It draws heaven's strength into my situation.

Rise Up Challenge: Speak one prayer of gratitude aloud today, even if the battle still feels active.

Rise in Victory

Day 240
Rise with Joy

August 28

"The joy of the Lord is your strength."
Nehemiah 8:10

Joy is not dependent on circumstance. It is the evidence of faith and the overflow of trust. When joy fills your heart, strength follows naturally.

Affirmation: My joy is my strength. I rise with gladness and gratitude.

Rise Up Challenge: Find one reason to smile today and thank God for it.

Day 241
Victory in Forgiveness

August 29

*"Bear with each other and forgive one another if
any of you has a grievance against someone.
Forgive as the Lord forgave you."*
Colossians 3:13

Forgiveness is freedom. It breaks the chains of bitterness and
opens the gates of peace. True victory is found in letting go.

Affirmation: I walk in forgiveness and live in freedom.

Rise Up Challenge: Pray for the strength to release any
lingering resentment or hurt.

Day 242
Rise in Renewal

August 30

*"Therefore, if anyone is in Christ, the new creation
has come: The old has gone, the new is here."*
2 Corinthians 5:17

Renewal is not about forgetting the past but being transformed
beyond it. Every mistake becomes a stepping stone toward
purpose.

Affirmation: I am renewed in Christ and made new each day.

Rise Up Challenge: Write down one truth about who you are in
Christ and repeat it throughout your day.

Day 243
Strength in Gratitude

August 31

*"Let us continually offer to God a sacrifice of praise,
the fruit of lips that openly profess His name."*
Hebrews 13:15

Gratitude shifts perspective. When you thank God through every season, you find strength that carries you through.

Affirmation: Gratitude strengthens me and magnifies God's goodness.

Rise Up Challenge: List five things you are thankful for, especially the ones you once took for granted.

Day 244
Rise with Vision

September 1

*"Write the vision and make it plain on tablets
so that a herald may run with it."*
Habakkuk 2:2

Vision gives direction to victory. God does not just call you to win; He calls you to build. Clarity comes when you write down what He has spoken.

Affirmation: My vision is clear, and my steps are guided by divine purpose.

Rise Up Challenge: Write down one goal or dream and ask God to guide your next step toward it.

Day 245
Faith That Finishes

September 2

"Do you not know that in a race all the runners run, but only one gets the prize? Run in such a way as to get the prize."
1 Corinthians 9:24

Finishing faith does not rush. It endures with steady resolve. Keep your eyes on Jesus, and you will cross every finish line with strength and grace.

Affirmation: I finish strong because my eyes are fixed on Christ.

Rise Up Challenge: Reflect on one area where you are nearing completion and thank God for endurance.

Day 246
Rise with Integrity

September 3

"The integrity of the upright guides them, but the unfaithful are destroyed by their duplicity."
Proverbs 11:3

Integrity is unseen victory. It builds strength when no one is watching. The man of honor wins long before the battle begins.

Affirmation: I walk in integrity and strength of character.

Rise Up Challenge: Make one decision today that honors truth, even if no one sees it.

Day 247
Victory in Unity

September 4

*"How good and pleasant it is when God's people
live together in unity."*
Psalm 133:1

Unity multiplies strength. Division drains it. God's presence
flows through harmony, and togetherness brings blessing.

Affirmation: I bring unity wherever I go, and God's peace flows
through me.

Rise Up Challenge: Reconnect or reconcile with someone
you've drifted from.

Day 248
Rise in Freedom

September 5

"So if the Son sets you free, you will be free indeed."
John 8:36

Freedom is not the absence of boundaries but the presence of peace. You are no longer chained to your past; you walk in the liberty of grace.

Affirmation: I live free in Christ, unbound and unburdened.

Rise Up Challenge: Do one thing today that celebrates your spiritual freedom.

Day 249
Victory That Glorifies God

September 6

"The Lord your God is with you, the Mighty Warrior who saves."
Zephaniah 3:17

Victory is not the end of your story; it is the evidence of His glory. Every win belongs to the One who carried you through.

Affirmation: My victory belongs to God, and my life reflects His glory.

Rise Up Challenge: End your day by thanking God for every victory He has already given you.

Day 250
Living Restored

September 7

"Our mouths were filled with laughter, our tongues with songs of joy... The Lord has done great things for us."
Psalm 126:2–3

This is your moment of laughter, joy, and lightness. You've walked the journey. Now live the testimony. Your restoration is real, radiant, and ready to ripple out into the world.

Affirmation: I live restored, radiant with joy, anchored in peace, and overflowing with grace.

Rise Up Challenge: Celebrate your transformation today. Write or speak aloud, "The Lord has done great things for me."

Day 251
Steady in the Light

September 8

"They will have no fear of bad news; their hearts are steadfast, trusting in the Lord."
Psalm 112:7

When your heart is healed, you no longer panic when life changes. Restoration brings a steady glow, grounded in peace, not circumstance.

Affirmation: My peace is steady. I trust God through every shift and season.

Rise Up Challenge: When something unexpected arises today, pause and say, "I am steady in the light."

Day 252
Restored Rhythm

September 9

"Learn from Me… for My yoke is easy and My burden is light."
Matthew 11:29–30

Restoration creates rhythm, the ease that comes from walking with God instead of rushing ahead of Him. When your soul aligns with His pace, peace flows naturally.

Affirmation: I move in divine rhythm. Peace sets my pace.

Rise Up Challenge: Slow down one routine task today. Breathe, savor, and do it with presence.

Day 253
Flourishing Faith

September 10

*"Planted in the house of the Lord, they will flourish
in the courts of our God."*
Psalm 92:13

You've outgrown survival. Now you're thriving. Flourishing faith means you no longer live in fear of what's next. You're rooted in trust and blooming in every area.

Affirmation: I am flourishing in faith. Growth and grace surround me.

Rise Up Challenge: Reflect on one area of your life that's flourishing, and thank God for the fruit.

Day 254
Restored Voice

September 11

"Let them give glory to the Lord and proclaim His praise in the islands."
Isaiah 42:12

Restoration gives your voice back. The same mouth that once spoke pain now proclaims praise. Your words are power. Use them to glorify and uplift.

Affirmation: My voice carries light. I speak life, not limitation.

Rise Up Challenge: Share one truth or encouragement today through your words, actions, or prayer.

Day 255
The Glow of Graceful Growth

September 12

*"I press on toward the goal to win the prize
for which God has called me heavenward in
Christ Jesus."*
Philippians 3:14

Graceful growth means you don't rush the process. You honor it and move forward without the weight of what once was.

Affirmation: I grow with grace. My past prepared me, but it no longer defines me.

Rise Up Challenge: Write down one lesson you've learned from your past that's helping you grow today.

Day 256
Restored Radiance

September 13

"Then you will look and be radiant; your heart will throb and swell with joy."
Isaiah 60:5

Restoration is visible. Others see the peace in your eyes, the steadiness in your spirit, and the strength in your presence. You are standing renewed from the inside out.

Affirmation: My restoration shines through every part of my being.

Rise Up Challenge: Look in the mirror today and speak this aloud: "This is what restoration looks like."

Day 257
Legacy of Light

September 14

"No one lights a lamp and puts it in a place where it will be hidden, or under a bowl. Instead they put it on its stand, so that those who come in may see the light."
Luke 11:33

Your restoration was never meant to stop with you. Each prayer, each hard-won victory, and each healed place becomes a legacy that strengthens those who follow.

Affirmation: I am leaving a legacy of light and love for those who follow.

Rise Up Challenge: Write a note, prayer, or message to the next generation, blessing them to walk in God's light.

Day 258
Sustained by Grace

September 15

"My grace is sufficient for you, for My power is made perfect in weakness."
2 Corinthians 12:9

Restoration doesn't mean perfection. It means presence. Grace sustains what strength cannot. When you lean into grace, you remain restored even when life wobbles.

Affirmation: Grace carries me daily. I don't strive, I surrender.

Rise Up Challenge: When you feel pressure today, pause and say, "Grace is enough for me right now."

Day 259
Restored Vision
and Focus

September 16

"Where there is no vision, the people perish."
Proverbs 29:18

Restoration renews your heart and sharpens your focus. God brings clarity where there was confusion and vision where there was discouragement.

Affirmation: My vision is clear, my focus is strong, and my eyes stay on God's purpose.

Rise Up Challenge: Write down your top three priorities for this season and invite God to be at the center of each.

Day 260
Faith-Filled Finishing

September 17

*"Let us hold unswervingly to the hope we profess,
for He who promised is faithful."*
Hebrews 10:23

Restoration includes endurance and finishing what God started in you. Faith-filled finishing means you stay steady until the promise is fulfilled.

Affirmation: I finish with faith, knowing God's promise is still unfolding.

Rise Up Challenge: Reflect on one goal or prayer still in progress. Thank God for the process, not just the outcome.

Day 261
The Glow of Humility

September 18

"Humble yourselves before the Lord,
and He will lift you up."
James 4:10

Humility is the hidden beauty of restoration. You shine not because you're elevated, but because you stayed surrendered. The glow of humility is gentle, powerful, and lasting.

Affirmation: I shine through humility. My heart remains soft before God.

Rise Up Challenge: Compliment or uplift someone else today. Celebrate their light as much as your own.

Day 262
Restored Routine

September 19

"Let all things be done decently and in order."
1 Corinthians 14:40

God blesses structure that flows with grace. Restored living means finding rhythm in your daily life that nourishes your body, mind, and spirit.

Affirmation: My daily rhythms reflect peace, order, and divine flow.

Rise Up Challenge: Create one simple morning or evening ritual that helps you feel aligned and calm.

Day 263
Restored Connection

September 20

"My command is this: Love each other
as I have loved you."
John 15:12

Restoration reconnects you to others through empathy, love, and understanding. God heals isolation by drawing you into divine community.

Affirmation: My relationships are restored through love, empathy, and grace.

Rise Up Challenge: Reach out to someone you haven't spoken to in a while. Reconnect from a place of love, not obligation.

Day 264
Overflowing Light

September 21

"If you spend yourselves in behalf of the hungry…
your light will rise in the darkness."
Isaiah 58:10

When you pour from overflow, not emptiness, your strength multiplies. Giving becomes your greatest joy, and your restoration blesses others effortlessly.

Affirmation: My light overflows. I give from abundance, not depletion.

Rise Up Challenge: Offer kindness today without expecting anything in return. Let your life be the offering.

Day 265
Peaceful Presence

September 22

"The Lord is near to all who call on Him, to all who call on Him in truth."
Psalm 145:18

Restoration deepens your presence. You stop striving and learn to rest. God's power moves through a quiet heart that listens more than it speaks. Peace comes through awareness, not escape.

Affirmation: I move through life with calm strength. My presence reflects God's peace.

Rise Up Challenge: Spend five minutes today in silence. Breathe slowly and let God's peace meet you there.

Day 266
Strength in Still Seasons

September 23

"The Lord will guide you always; He will satisfy your needs in a sun-scorched land and will strengthen your frame."
Isaiah 58:11

Even when life slows down, God is still working. Waiting is disciplined strength. Still seasons form endurance, not apathy.

Affirmation: My stillness is power. I trust God to move even when I stand still.

Rise Up Challenge: Resist the urge to force progress. Choose one thing to leave in God's hands today.

Day 267
Power of Gratitude

September 24

"Let them give thanks to the Lord for His unfailing love and His wonderful deeds for mankind."
Psalm 107:8

Gratitude turns battle scars into badges of honor. When you thank God in every season, you transform trials into testimonies. Gratitude does not ignore pain. It declares victory in the middle of it.

Affirmation: Gratitude keeps my heart strong and my faith focused.

Rise Up Challenge: Write three things you are grateful for right now, even if they stretched you to grow.

Day 268
Purpose in Peace

September 25

"You will keep in perfect peace those whose minds are steadfast, because they trust in You."
Isaiah 26:3

True power is quiet confidence. Peace isn't the absence of battle but the certainty of victory. When you walk with purpose, peace becomes your anchor in every storm.

Affirmation: My peace is anchored in God's promises. My purpose stands firm.

Rise Up Challenge: When tension rises today, choose peace over pressure. Let calm lead the way.

Day 269
Strength in the Struggle

September 26

"I can do all things through Christ who strengthens me."
Philippians 4:13

Strength isn't proven by what you lift, but by what you carry with grace. Even when you feel stretched thin, God is strengthening your spirit for the climb ahead.

Affirmation: My strength comes from Christ within me. I rise through every challenge.

Rise Up Challenge: Do one thing today that requires perseverance, not perfection.

Day 270
Strength Renewed

September 27

*"They that hope in the Lord will renew their strength;
they will soar on wings like eagles; they will run and not
grow weary, they will walk and not be faint."*
Isaiah 40:31

Victory begins with renewed strength. When your faith feels
tired, remember that your power isn't self-made. It's
Spirit-breathed. God lifts those who lean on Him.

Affirmation: My strength is restored daily by God's Spirit.

Rise Up Challenge: Take ten minutes today to pause and
breathe deeply in prayer. Let renewal rise from within.

Day 271
The Battle Belongs to the Lord

September 28

"The battle is the Lord's."
1 Samuel 17:47

True victory is surrender. Courage doesn't always roar; it sometimes waits while God works.

Affirmation: I am still while God fights for me.

Rise Up Challenge: Release one battle to God today. Write it down and declare it finished in His hands.

Day 272
Steadfast Under Pressure

September 29

"Let us not grow weary in doing good, for at the proper time we will reap a harvest if we do not give up."
Galatians 6:9

Pressure proves purpose. God shapes champions through endurance, not ease.

Affirmation: I persevere with peace and purpose.

Rise Up Challenge: When frustration hits, whisper: God is forming something eternal in me.

Day 273
Victory in Vision

September 30

"The plans of the diligent lead surely
to abundance."
Proverbs 21:5

A warrior without vision drifts. Clarity is power. God blesses the man who moves with divine direction.

Affirmation: My vision is clear. My steps are steady.

Rise Up Challenge: Write one goal connected to your calling and pray over it.

Day 274
Courage to Stand Alone

October 1

"Be on your guard; stand firm in the faith; be courageous; be strong."
1 Corinthians 16:13

Standing alone with God outweighs standing with the crowd without Him.

Affirmation: I stand firm even when others fall away.

Rise Up Challenge: Choose conviction over comfort in one area today.

Day 275
Faith That Conquers Fear

October 2

"When I am afraid, I put my trust in You."
Psalm 56:3

Fear flees when faith stands tall. Courage is confidence in God's covering.

Affirmation: Fear bows to my faith.

Rise Up Challenge: Face one fear today through prayer and movement.

Day 276
Unbroken Spirit

October 3

*"The Lord is close to the brokenhearted and saves
those who are crushed in spirit."*
Psalm 34:18

Broken seasons shape a man in ways comfort never could. When
your spirit feels pressed, stretched, or worn thin, God draws near
with steady hands, forming strength deep within you.

Affirmation: My spirit is unbreakable because God holds it
together.

Rise Up Challenge: Reach out to someone hurting and remind
them of God's nearness.

Day 277
Purpose in Every Step

October 4

"The Lord makes firm the steps of the one who delights in Him."
Psalm 37:23

Each step matters when it's guided by God. Even detours become destiny when faith directs your path.

Affirmation: My steps are ordered and purposeful.

Rise Up Challenge: Walk intentionally today in both spirit and action, thanking God for His direction.

Day 278
Faith That Echoes

October 5

"Their faith and love became known everywhere."
1 Thessalonians 1:8

Faith leaves a legacy. What you believe today shapes what others will see tomorrow.

Affirmation: My faith echoes beyond my lifetime.

Rise Up Challenge: Encourage someone younger in faith with your testimony.

Day 279
Victory Through Praise

October 6

"Let everything that has breath praise the Lord."
Psalm 150:6

Praise is the roar of victory. It confuses the enemy and centers your soul in joy.

Affirmation: My praise carries power.

Rise Up Challenge: Start and end your day with five minutes of pure praise.

Day 280
Victory Through Grace

October 7

"The Lord is my strength and my shield."
Psalm 28:7

Grace fuels victory. When you lay your weakness before God, He forms strength in its place. You stand secure because of Him.

Affirmation: Grace makes me victorious.

Rise Up Challenge: Thank God aloud for one weakness He's turned into strength.

Day 281
Armor of Light

October 8

*"Let us put aside the deeds of darkness and put on
the armor of light."*
Romans 13:12

Light is your uniform. When clothed in righteousness, you walk
protected and radiant.

Affirmation: I am armored in light and truth.

Rise Up Challenge: Pray through each piece of spiritual armor
from Ephesians 6.

Day 282
Hearts That Heal

October 9

"Above all else, guard your heart, for everything you do flows from it."
Proverbs 4:23

A healed heart carries holy power. Guarding your heart doesn't mean hiding it; it means giving it fully to God.

Affirmation: My heart is whole and guarded by grace.

Rise Up Challenge: Write down three things that keep your heart peaceful and commit to them this week.

Day 283
Rise in Victory

October 10

"But thanks be to God! He gives us the victory through our Lord Jesus Christ."
1 Corinthians 15:57

This is the moment you rise. Every battle has built your belief, and every challenge has refined your courage. You now walk in victory, strong, steadfast, and fearless in Christ.

Affirmation: I rise in victory, fully alive in Christ's power.

Rise Up Challenge: End your day by declaring: The battle is won, the victory is mine through Him.

Day 284
Unshakeable Foundation

October 11

"For no one can lay any foundation other than the one already laid, which is Jesus Christ."
1 Corinthians 3:11

When your foundation is Christ, no storm can shake you. Strength doesn't come from standing tall. It comes from being rooted deep.

Affirmation: My faith stands firm because Christ is my foundation.

Rise Up Challenge: Pray today for God to strengthen your spiritual foundation beneath every area of your life.

Day 285
Victorious Mindset

October 12

"Do not conform to the pattern of this world, but be transformed by the renewing of your mind."
Romans 12:2

Victory starts in your thoughts. When your mind aligns with God's truth, defeat loses its grip.

Affirmation: My thoughts are renewed with truth and power.

Rise Up Challenge: Replace one negative thought today with a declaration of victory.

Day 286
Endurance That Overcomes

October 13

"But you, brothers and sisters, do not grow weary in doing what is good."
2 Thessalonians 3:13

Endurance is the language of victory. God rewards those who keep going, even when no one is watching.

Affirmation: I endure with strength, knowing my harvest is coming.

Rise Up Challenge: Stay committed to one good habit today that strengthens your faith.

Day 287
Faith That Guards Peace

October 14

"And the peace of God, which transcends all understanding, will guard your hearts and your minds in Christ Jesus."
Philippians 4:7

The peace of God surrounds you like a guard at the gate. It steadies your heart and sharpens your mind. In Christ, you stand firm.

Affirmation: God's peace guards my heart and mind.

Rise Up Challenge: Guard your peace today by refusing to react to negativity.

Day 288

Rising Through Adversity

October 15

"We are hard pressed on every side, but not crushed; perplexed, but not in despair."
2 Corinthians 4:8

Adversity reveals resilience. Every time you rise after being knocked down, heaven applauds your endurance.

Affirmation: I rise stronger through every challenge.

Rise Up Challenge: Reflect on a past hardship and thank God for how it grew you.

Day 289
Faith That Speaks Truth

October 16

"Therefore each of you must put off falsehood and speak truthfully to your neighbor."
Ephesians 4:25

True faith speaks truth, even when it's uncomfortable. God honors those whose words reflect His character.

Affirmation: My words align with God's truth and integrity.

Rise Up Challenge: Speak a truth in love today, even if it's difficult.

Day 290
Victory Over Temptation

October 17

"No temptation has overtaken you except what is common to mankind. And God is faithful; He will not let you be tempted beyond what you can bear.
1 Corinthians 10:13

Temptation tests strength, not weakness. Every victory over temptation builds spiritual muscle.

Affirmation: God gives me strength to overcome every temptation.

Rise Up Challenge: When temptation strikes, pray before reacting. Choose discipline over desire.

Day 291
Hope That Anchors

October 18

"We have this hope as an anchor for the soul, firm and secure."
Hebrews 6:19

Hope holds steady when waves crash. It's not denial; it's trust in divine timing.

Affirmation: My hope anchors my soul in peace.

Rise Up Challenge: Remind yourself of one promise God has fulfilled in your life.

Day 292
Quiet Strength

October 19

"In repentance and rest is your salvation, in quietness and trust is your strength."
Isaiah 30:15

Stillness is strength under control. Warriors who rest in God fight from a place of peace.

Affirmation: I am strong in stillness and confident in God's sovereignty.

Rise Up Challenge: Spend five quiet minutes today in silence before God.

Day 293
Faith That Multiplies Courage

October 20

"Be strong and very courageous. Be careful to obey all the law My servant Moses gave you."
Joshua 1:7

Courage grows through obedience. When you walk God's way, fear fades into faith.

Affirmation: I am strong and courageous through obedience to God.

Rise Up Challenge: Take one obedient step today toward what God's been calling you to do.

Day 294
The Power of Prayer

October 21

"The prayer of a righteous person is powerful and effective."
James 5:16

Prayer isn't the backup plan. It's the battle plan. Heaven moves when you kneel in faith.

Affirmation: My prayers are powerful and heard by God.

Rise Up Challenge: Pray intentionally for someone else's breakthrough today.

Day 295
Light in Darkness

October 22

"The light shines in the darkness, and the darkness has not overcome it."
John 1:5

Darkness never wins when light stands firm. God's presence in you pushes back every shadow.

Affirmation: God's light in me overcomes all darkness.

Rise Up Challenge: Be a light today where negativity or despair try to linger.

Day 296
Strength in Unity

October 23

"Two are better than one, because they have a good return for their labor."
Ecclesiastes 4:9

Unity builds victory. Lone lions are strong, but a pride moving together is unstoppable.

Affirmation: I build unity through grace and humility.

Rise Up Challenge: Encourage collaboration or peace within your circle today.

Day 297
Standing on Promises

October 24

"For no matter how many promises God has made, they are 'Yes' in Christ."
2 Corinthians 1:20

God's promises never fail. Every "yes" in His Word anchors your faith in something eternal.

Affirmation: God's promises are my foundation and fuel.

Rise Up Challenge: Write down three promises from Scripture that remind you of your strength in Him.

Day 298
Rise with Purpose

October 25

*"For we are God's handiwork, created in Christ
Jesus to do good works."*
Ephesians 2:10

Purpose is the reason behind every victory. When you rise in
purpose, you move with divine confidence and holy clarity.

Affirmation: I walk in my God-given purpose with focus and
strength.

Rise Up Challenge: Take one bold action today that aligns with
your purpose and honors God.

Day 299
Victory That Endures

October 26

"The Lord is my strength and my song; He has
become my salvation."
Psalm 118:14

Enduring victory is not loud. It is steady, patient, and anchored in trust. What lasts is not built in haste but in faithfulness. You are still standing because God has been strengthening you all along.

Affirmation: My victory endures because God sustains me.

Rise Up Challenge: Identify one habit that has helped you persevere and commit to continue it this week.

Day 300
Strength Beyond Self

October 27

"My flesh and my heart may fail, but God is the strength of my heart and my portion forever."
Psalm 73:26

True strength is not self-made. It flows from reliance on God rather than resistance to Him. When you lean on Him, you stand stronger than you ever could alone.

Affirmation: God is my strength, not my striving.

Rise Up Challenge: Ask God today where He wants to carry you instead of you carrying everything yourself.

Day 301
Victory in Trust

October 28

"The Lord is good, a refuge in times of trouble.
He cares for those who trust in Him."
Nahum 1:7

Trust is the quiet confidence that God is working even when you cannot see results. Victory deepens when control is released and faith takes the lead.

Affirmation: I trust God completely with my life and future.

Rise Up Challenge: Release one worry today by placing it intentionally in God's hands.

Day 302
Peace That Guards

October 29

*"Great peace have those who love Your law, and
nothing causes them to stumble."*
Psalm 119:165

Peace is protection. When God's peace guards you, fear loses
authority and clarity returns. Victory is sustained when peace
stands watch.

Affirmation: God's peace guards my heart and mind.

Rise Up Challenge: Pause before reacting today and choose
peace as your response.

Day 303
Strength in Obedience

October 30

"Those who obey the Lord lack nothing."
Psalm 34:10

Obedience is strength in action. Each yes to God reinforces your foundation and moves you forward with purpose and clarity.

Affirmation: I grow stronger through obedience to God.

Rise Up Challenge: Follow through today on something God has already asked you to do.

Day 304
Victory Through Humility

October 31

"God opposes the proud but shows favor to the humble."
Psalm 4:8

Humility keeps victory grounded. It protects your heart and keeps your strength aligned with God's will rather than self-glory.

Affirmation: I walk in humility and receive God's grace.

Rise Up Challenge: Acknowledge God's hand in a recent success and give Him thanks.

Day 305
Faith That Remains

November 1

"Now faith is confidence in what we hope for."
Hebrews 11:1

Faith that remains does not waver with circumstances. It stays rooted in promise, steady through change, and confident in God's faithfulness.

Affirmation: My faith remains strong and confident in God.

Rise Up Challenge: Write down one promise you are still standing on and reaffirm your trust in it.

Day 306
Steady in Victory

November 2

"The Lord gives strength to His people; the Lord blesses His people with peace."
Psalm 29:11

Victory matures when steadiness replaces urgency. God strengthens those who remain faithful without rushing the process.

Affirmation: I remain steady, strong, and confident in God's victory.

Rise Up Challenge: Move through today without rushing. Let strength come from steadiness.

Day 307
Victory in Perseverance

November 3

"But as for you, be strong and do not give up, for your work will be rewarded."
2 Chronicles 15:7

Perseverance is quiet strength that refuses to quit. Even when progress feels slow, God is working beneath the surface. Victory belongs to those who remain faithful through the waiting.

Affirmation: I persevere with confidence, knowing God is at work.

Rise Up Challenge: Stay committed to one good practice today, even if motivation feels low.

Day 308
Strength Through Faithfulness

November 4

"Moreover, it is required of stewards that they be found faithful."
1 Corinthians 4:2

Faithfulness is victory lived daily. God values consistency over visibility. Each faithful step strengthens your walk and produces lasting fruit.

Affirmation: My faithfulness honors God and produces lasting strength.

Rise Up Challenge: Complete one responsibility today with excellence and integrity.

Day 309
Victory in Clarity

November 5

"The Lord gives wisdom."
Proverbs 2:6

Clarity is a form of victory. When God removes confusion, direction becomes steady and decisions feel lighter. Wisdom strengthens every step forward.

Affirmation: God grants me wisdom and clear direction.

Rise Up Challenge: Ask God for clarity before making any decision today.

Day 310

Strength Anchored in Hope

November 6

"Hope does not put us to shame."
Romans 5:5

Hope strengthens the heart when outcomes remain unseen. It anchors your spirit in God's promises and keeps you moving forward with courage.

Affirmation: My hope is secure and strengthens my faith.

Rise Up Challenge: Write down one hope you are holding onto and thank God for it.

Day 311
Victory Through Trust

November 7

"The Lord is trustworthy in all He does."
Psalm 145:13

Trust grows when you remember God's faithfulness. Victory deepens when fear is replaced with confidence in who He is.

Affirmation: I trust God fully with every part of my life.

Rise Up Challenge: Release control over one situation and place it in God's care.

Day 312
Strength That Stands Firm

November 8

"Be strong in the Lord and in His mighty power."
Ephesians 6:10

Standing firm does not mean standing alone. God's strength surrounds you, supports you, and keeps you grounded through every challenge.

Affirmation: I stand firm in God's strength, not my own.

Rise Up Challenge: Face one challenge today with confidence instead of hesitation.

Day 313
Victory in Peaceful Confidence

November 9

*"In peace I will lie down and sleep, for You alone,
Lord, make me dwell in safety."*
Psalm 4:8

Confidence rooted in peace is powerful. When your mind stays fixed on God, anxiety loosens its grip and calm strength takes over.

Affirmation: My confidence is calm, steady, and rooted in God.

Rise Up Challenge: Redirect anxious thoughts today by focusing on one truth from Scripture.

Day 314
Strength for the Journey Ahead

November 10

"The Lord goes before you."
Deuteronomy 31:8

God prepares the path before you step onto it. Victory continues as you trust Him with what comes next, knowing you never walk alone.

Affirmation: God goes before me and strengthens my path.

Rise Up Challenge: Pray over what lies ahead and step forward with confidence.

Day 315
Victory Through Patience

November 11

"Be still before the Lord and wait patiently for Him."
Psalm 37:7

Patience is strength under control. Victory is often formed in waiting, where trust deepens and faith matures without rushing the outcome.

Affirmation: I wait with patience, trusting God's perfect timing.

Rise Up Challenge: Practice patience today by slowing one response or decision.

Day 316
Thankful and Steady

November 12

*"I will praise God's name in song and glorify Him
with thanksgiving."*
Psalm 69:30

Gratitude strengthens the soul. When you acknowledge God's goodness, your perspective shifts and peace settles in.

Affirmation: Gratitude strengthens my heart and steadies my faith.

Rise Up Challenge: Thank God for one answered prayer you once waited for.

Day 317
Victory Over Discouragement

November 13

*"Why, my soul, are you downcast? Put your hope
in God."*
Psalm 42:11

Discouragement fades when hope is restored. God lifts your spirit when you choose to remember who He is rather than what you feel.

Affirmation: My hope rises above discouragement.

Rise Up Challenge: Replace one negative thought today with a spoken truth.

Day 318
Strength Through Dependence

November 14

"Cast all your anxiety on Him because He cares for you."
1 Peter 5:7

True strength grows when you stop striving and start depending.
God meets you fully where your effort ends.

Affirmation: I depend on God's grace for daily strength.

Rise Up Challenge: Ask God for help before acting on one task
today.

Day 319
Victory in Quiet Obedience

November 15

"Blessed are those who hear the word of God and obey it."
Luke 11:28

Obedience does not need applause to be powerful. Quiet faithfulness carries lasting victory.

Affirmation: I walk in obedience with a willing heart.

Rise Up Challenge: Follow through on one instruction God has already given you.

Day 320

Strength That Endures

November 16

"God is our refuge and strength, an ever-present help in trouble."
Psalm 46:1

Endurance is built through trust. God strengthens you not just for today, but for everything still ahead.

Affirmation: God's strength sustains me through every season.

Rise Up Challenge: Reflect on how God has strengthened you over time.

Day 321
Victory Through Faith

November 17

*"This is the victory that has overcome the world,
even our faith."*
1 John 5:4

Faith is not passive. It actively overcomes fear, doubt, and resistance when you choose to believe God's promises.

Affirmation: My faith overcomes every obstacle.

Rise Up Challenge: Declare one promise of God aloud today.

Day 322
Strength Rooted in Trust

November 18

"Trust in the Lord with all your heart."
Proverbs 3:5

Trust steadies the heart. When your confidence rests in God, fear loses its grip and peace leads the way.

Affirmation: My trust in God keeps me steady and strong.

Rise Up Challenge: Surrender one concern today and choose trust instead.

Rise in Victory

Day 323
Strength in Hope

November 19

*"May the God of hope fill you with all joy and
peace as you trust in Him."*
Romans 15:13

Hope strengthens the heart when circumstances feel uncertain.
Trusting God allows peace and joy to rise even before outcomes
change.

Affirmation: Hope fills my heart as I trust God fully.

Rise Up Challenge: Write down one situation where you are
choosing hope over worry.

Day 324
Victory Through Consistency

November 20

"Being confident of this, that He who began a good work in you will carry it on to completion."
Philippians 1:6

Consistency builds quiet strength. Small faithful choices, repeated daily, lead to lasting victory.

Affirmation: I remain steady and faithful in what God has given me.

Rise Up Challenge: Complete one routine task today with excellence and intention.

Day 325

Strength in Clarity

November 21

*"If any of you lacks wisdom, you should ask God,
who gives generously to all."*
James 1:5

Clarity brings confidence. God provides understanding when you
seek Him rather than rushing decisions.

Affirmation: God's wisdom brings clarity to my path.

Rise Up Challenge: Ask God for guidance before making a
decision today.

Day 326

Victory in Peaceful Resolve

November 22

"Let the peace of Christ rule in your hearts."
Colossians 3:15

Peace grows when your mind stays fixed on truth. Steadfast resolve keeps anxiety from leading.

Affirmation: My mind is steady, and my peace is secure.

Rise Up Challenge: Redirect your thoughts when distraction or worry arises.

Day 327
Faithful to the Finish

November 23

"Well done, good and faithful servant."
Matthew 25:21

Faithfulness matters more than recognition. God sees every act of obedience and honors a steady heart. Even when no one applauds, Heaven records your consistency. What you do in quiet devotion is shaping eternal reward.

Affirmation: I remain faithful in every responsibility God entrusts to me.

Rise Up Challenge: Serve faithfully today without seeking acknowledgment.

Day 328
Trust That Holds Under Pressure

November 24

"Those who trust in the Lord are like Mount Zion, which cannot be shaken but endures forever."
Psalm 125:1

Trust deepens when you remember God's faithfulness. His promises remain secure, regardless of timing.

Affirmation: I trust God because He is faithful.

Rise Up Challenge: Recall one promise God has already fulfilled and thank Him.

Day 329
Thankful Strength

November 25

"Enter His gates with thanksgiving and His courts with praise; give thanks to Him and praise His name."
Psalm 100:4

Gratitude anchors the heart. Thankfulness shifts focus from what's missing to what God has provided.

Affirmation: Gratitude grounds my heart in truth.

Rise Up Challenge: Express thanks to someone who has supported you.

Day 330

Victory Through Endurance

November 26

"Therefore we do not lose heart. Though outwardly we are wasting away, yet inwardly we are being renewed day by day."
2 Corinthians 4:16

Endurance reveals maturity. God strengthens those who continue forward without giving up.

Affirmation: I endure with confidence and faith.

Rise Up Challenge: Keep going in one area where you've felt tempted to stop.

Day 331
Strength Through Obedience

November 27

*"Blessed are all who fear the Lord, who walk in
obedience to Him."*
Psalm 128:1

Obedience strengthens faith by aligning your steps with God's
direction. Victory follows when you choose His way over your
own.

Affirmation: I walk in obedience with confidence and trust.

Rise Up Challenge: Obey one prompting from God today
without hesitation.

Day 332

Victory in Still Confidence

November 28

"The fruit of that righteousness will be peace; its effect will be quietness and confidence forever."
Isaiah 32:17

Confidence rooted in God does not need noise or validation. Quiet trust produces steady strength.

Affirmation: My confidence rests securely in God.

Rise Up Challenge: Release one worry today and replace it with trust.

Day 333
Strength Through Integrity

November 29

"Whoever walks in integrity walks securely."
Proverbs 10:9

Integrity leads with clarity. When your choices reflect truth, strength follows naturally.

Affirmation: Integrity guides my decisions and actions.

Rise Up Challenge: Choose honesty today, even when it costs convenience.

Day 334
Victory in Discipline

November 30

"No discipline seems pleasant at the time, but later it produces a harvest."
Hebrews 12:11

Discipline prepares you for lasting victory. What you practice now shapes the strength you walk in later.

Affirmation: Discipline strengthens me for what God has prepared.

Rise Up Challenge: Commit to one healthy discipline and follow through today.

Day 335
Strength in Trust

December 1

"Trust in the Lord forever, for the Lord, the Lord Himself, is the Rock eternal."
Isaiah 26:4

Trust brings peace where control fails. God honors surrendered steps with steady guidance.

Affirmation: I trust God with every step forward.

Rise Up Challenge: Pray over one plan and release the outcome to God.

Day 336
Humble and Lifted

December 2

"The reward for humility and fear of the Lord is riches and honor and life."
Proverbs 22:4

Humility opens the door to elevation. God strengthens those who remain teachable.

Affirmation: I walk humbly, trusting God to lead.

Rise Up Challenge: Acknowledge God's role in one success today.

Day 337
Strength in Purpose

December 3

"The Lord will fulfill His purpose for me."
Psalm 138:8

Purpose anchors you when progress feels slow. God completes what He begins. Slow progress still carries power. Your assignment is unfolding exactly as it should.

Affirmation: God's purpose is active in my life.

Rise Up Challenge: Write one purpose-driven goal and commit it to prayer.

Day 338
Peace That Rules My Heart

December 4

"Now may the Lord of peace Himself give you peace at all times and in every way."
2 Thessalonians 3:16

Peace is a decision guided by faith. When peace rules, confusion loses authority.

Affirmation: Peace governs my heart and decisions.

Rise Up Challenge: Choose peace over reaction in one situation today.

Day 339
Steady Through Trust

December 5

*"Commit your way to the Lord; trust in Him
and He will act."*
Psalm 37:5

Victory is sustained when trust replaces control. God strengthens those who rely on His wisdom rather than their own.

Affirmation: I trust God completely, even when the path is unclear.

Rise Up Challenge: Surrender one decision today and invite God to lead it fully.

Day 340
Strength Without Striving

December 6

*"Truly my soul finds rest in God; my salvation
comes from Him."*
Psalm 62:1

You were never meant to force victory. Strength flows when you receive what God freely gives.

Affirmation: I receive strength from God without striving.

Rise Up Challenge: Pause before pushing forward today and ask God for His strength instead.

Day 341
Victory in Patience

December 7

"Wait for the Lord; be strong and take heart."
Psalm 27:14

Patience builds endurance. Waiting on God is not weakness but disciplined trust.

Affirmation: Patience strengthens my faith and steadies my spirit.

Rise Up Challenge: Practice patience in one situation that usually tests you.

Day 342
Strength in Right Choices

December 8

"The way of the righteous leads to life."
Proverbs 12:28

Right choices create lasting victory. Obedience today shapes peace tomorrow.

Affirmation: I choose what is right, even when it is difficult.

Rise Up Challenge: Make one choice today that aligns with God's truth.

Day 343
Clarity Covered in Peace

December 9

"For God is not a God of confusion but of peace."
1 Corinthians 14:33

Clarity brings calm. When God leads, confusion gives way to confidence. When your heart is anchored in Him, your steps become clear, firm, and unshaken.

Affirmation: God brings clarity and peace to my decisions.

Rise Up Challenge: Remove one source of unnecessary distraction today.

Day 344

Strength That Perseveres

December 10

"Blessed is the one who perseveres under trial…"
James 1:12

Perseverance produces maturity. God strengthens those who stay faithful through pressure.

Affirmation: I remain steadfast and grounded through every trial.

Rise Up Challenge: Keep going in one area where quitting feels tempting.

Day 345
Victory in Gratitude

December 11

"Give thanks to the Lord, for He is good."
Psalm 107:1

Gratitude guards the heart. Victory lasts longer when it is carried with thanks. Gratitude keeps you grounded when success could lift you too high.

Affirmation: Gratitude keeps my heart strong and focused.

Rise Up Challenge: Thank God today for something you once struggled with.

Day 346
Strength to Finish Well

December 12

"Therefore, my dear brothers and sisters, stand firm. Let nothing move you. Always give yourselves fully to the work of the Lord..."
1 Corinthians 15:58

Finishing well requires endurance. God honors those who stay faithful until the end.

Affirmation: I have strength to finish what God has entrusted to me.

Rise Up Challenge: Take one intentional step today toward completing a long-term goal.

Day 347
Strength in Discipline

December 13

"Whoever loves discipline loves knowledge."
Proverbs 12:1

Discipline protects what victory produces. Consistent habits keep strength from slipping away. Is it in the daily choices that character is forged and endurance is built.

Affirmation: Discipline strengthens my life and guards my growth.

Rise Up Challenge: Commit to one small discipline today and follow through.

Day 348
Victory in Integrity

December 14

*"The righteous who walks in his integrity, blessed
are his children after him!"*
Proverbs 20:7

Integrity directs your steps even when no one is watching. God honors truth lived quietly.

Affirmation: Integrity guides my choices and anchors my character.

Rise Up Challenge: Choose honesty today even if it costs you comfort.

Day 349
Faithful With What I'm Given

December 15

"Whoever can be trusted with very little can also be trusted with much."
Luke 16:10

Faithfulness is strength over time. God values consistency more than recognition.

Affirmation: I remain faithful to what God has entrusted to me.

Rise Up Challenge: Complete one responsibility today with excellence and focus.

Day 350
Grounded Before Glory

December 16

"Humble yourselves under God's mighty hand, that He may lift you up in due time."
1 Peter 5:6

Humility keeps victory clean. When pride fades, God's favor increases. Stay grounded before glory, and Heaven will trust you with more.

Affirmation: I walk humbly and rely fully on God's grace.

Rise Up Challenge: Serve someone today without seeking recognition.

Day 351
Strength That Guards Peace

December 17

*"You will go out in joy and be led
forth in peace..."*
Isaiah 55:12

Peace protects strength. A settled spirit keeps victory steady.

Affirmation: God's peace guards my strength and focus.

Rise Up Challenge: Refuse to engage in unnecessary conflict today.

Day 352
Victory in Self-Control

December 18

"A person without self-control is like a city with broken walls."
Proverbs 25:28

Self-control secures what victory builds. Strength grows when restraint leads. A disciplined spirit protects the ground God has already given you.

Affirmation: I lead my actions with wisdom and self-control.

Rise Up Challenge: Pause before reacting today and choose restraint.

Day 353
Strength in Obedient Steps

December 19

"Those who fear Him lack nothing."
Psalm 34:9

Every obedient step builds spiritual endurance. Discipline today becomes authority tomorrow. Those who walk in obedience walk in strength.

Affirmation: My obedience strengthens my walk with God.

Rise Up Challenge: Act immediately on one clear prompting from God today.

Day 354

Endurance That Receives the Promise

December 20

"You need to persevere so that when you have done the will of God, you will receive what He has promised."
Hebrews 10:36

Endurance carries victory across the finish line. God rewards those who stay faithful. Those who refuse to quit are the ones who see the promise fulfilled.

Affirmation: I endure with confidence in God's promises.

Rise Up Challenge: Keep going today where progress feels slow.

Day 355
Steady to the Finish

December 21

*"Let us run with perseverance the race
marked out for us."*
Hebrews 12:1

Victory requires steady steps, not sudden bursts. Faithfulness in the final stretch matters just as much as strength at the start.

Affirmation: I finish this journey with perseverance and focus.

Rise Up Challenge: Reflect on how far you've come and thank God for sustaining you.

Day 356
Strength in Reflection

December 22

"Remember the wonders He has done."
Psalm 105:5

Looking back reveals God's faithfulness. Reflection strengthens confidence for what lies ahead.

Affirmation: Remembering God's faithfulness strengthens my faith.

Rise Up Challenge: Write down three moments this year where God carried you through.

Day 357
Peace Before Promise

December 23

"Peace I leave with you; My peace I give you."
John 14:27

Before every promise fulfilled, God offers peace. Calm your heart and prepare to receive.

Affirmation: I rest in God's peace as I wait with expectation.

Rise Up Challenge: Release one lingering worry into God's hands today.

Day 358

Hope Is Born

December 24

"For unto us a Child is born, unto us a Son is given."
Isaiah 9:6

Christmas Eve reminds you that hope enters quietly but changes everything. God's greatest victory arrived humbly, wrapped in promise.

Affirmation: Hope lives in me because Christ has come.

Rise Up Challenge: Pause tonight and thank God for the hope He placed in your life through Jesus.

Day 359
Victory Has a Name

December 25

"The Word became flesh and made His dwelling among us."
John 1:14

Christmas is the celebration of victory fulfilled. Jesus is the promise kept, the Savior given, the victory secured forever.

Affirmation: Jesus is my victory, today and always.

Rise Up Challenge: Celebrate Christ today by honoring Him with gratitude, joy, and worship.

Day 360
Gratitude That Grounds Me

December 26

*"Those who sacrifice thank offerings honor Me,
and to the blameless I will show My salvation."*
Psalm 50:23

Gratitude keeps victory grounded. Thankfulness turns reflection into renewal. A grateful heart remembers where it started and honors the One who carrier it through.

Affirmation: Gratitude strengthens my heart and steadies my spirit.

Rise Up Challenge: Thank God today for both the victories and the lessons.

Day 361
Renewed for What's Ahead

December 27

"Forget the former things; do not dwell on the past."
Isaiah 43:18

God prepares you for what's next by releasing what's behind. Renewal makes room for new strength.

Affirmation: I release the past and step forward renewed.

Rise Up Challenge: Let go of one thing from this year that no longer serves you.

Day 362
Strength for the Future

December 28

"I will instruct you and teach you in the way you should go; I will counsel you with My loving eye on you."
Psalm 32:8

What God started, He will complete. Confidence in His plan gives peace for the future.

Affirmation: God is faithful to complete what He began in me.

Rise Up Challenge: Pray confidently over the coming year and invite God to lead it.

Day 363
Victory in Trust

December 29

*"Trust in the Lord and do good; dwell in
the land and enjoy safe pasture."*
Psalm 37:3

Trust anchors you as you step forward. Victory grows where
surrender leads. Trust deeply, and you will walk forward
without hesitation.

Affirmation: I trust God fully with what lies ahead.

Rise Up Challenge: Commit one specific area of your future to
God today.

Day 364
Prepared to Rise Again

December 30

"The One who calls you is faithful, and He will do it."
1 Thessalonians 5:24

Every ending prepares a new beginning. God equips you to rise again with wisdom and strength.

Affirmation: I am prepared for what God is calling me into next.

Rise Up Challenge: Reflect on one way God has grown you this year.

Day 365
Rise Complete

December 31

"I have fought the good fight, I have finished the race, I have kept the faith."
2 Timothy 4:7

You have finished this journey stronger than you began. Faith carried you. God shaped you. Victory remains with you.

Affirmation: I stand strong, faithful, and victorious in Christ.

Rise Up Challenge: End this year by declaring aloud, "God has been faithful, and I rise in victory."

Closing Reflection
Fully Grounded & Standing Victorious

Take a steady breath.
You made it.

You have walked through fire and stood firm when it would have been easier to fall back. You faced resistance, learned endurance, and chose faith when comfort was an option. What began as a call to stand has become a way of life rooted in truth, refined by faith, and proven through perseverance.
Every prayer you prayed. Every moment you stayed when walking away felt easier. Every choice to rise instead of retreat. All of it shaped the man you are now. You learned that strength is not loud. It is steady. It is disciplined. It is anchored in God.

Your foundation was laid on truth.

Your faith was refined through pressure.

Your courage was forged under fire.

Your purpose became clear through obedience.

And now, you stand in victory.

You no longer fight for position. You stand in authority.

You no longer react to fear. You respond with wisdom.

You no longer chase strength. You walk in it.

This is what victory looks like. Not pride, but confidence. Not noise, but presence. Not striving, but faith in motion.

———•———

You are no longer preparing to rise. You have risen.

Carry this strength forward.
Stand firm when the world shifts.
Lead with integrity when no one is watching.
Trust God when the path requires patience.
You are living proof that faith works.
You are evidence that endurance produces power.
You are a man grounded in truth and standing in victory.
This is not the end of your journey.
This is the posture you now walk in.

Stand strong.
Walk boldly.
Remain faithful.

Final Blessing

Holy Strength, Holy Stand

May your heart remain anchored in truth.
May your faith stand firm when pressure rises and storms surround you. May you walk with strength that is steady, courage that is disciplined, and humility that keeps you aligned with God's will. May your foundation stay unshaken, your spirit remain resolved, and your purpose never drift.

When you look back, may you see not the battles that tried to break you, but the strength God built within you through them. When you look ahead, may you move with the confidence of one who knows the victory is already secured in Christ. And when you stand still, may you sense the quiet assurance of Heaven, knowing you are covered, called, and held. You were not shaped by comfort. You were forged by truth. You were strengthened through resistance. And you were raised to stand with faith that endures.

Stand firm. Walk forward. Remain faithful.
You are rising in victory, today, tomorrow, and
for all the days God has set before you.

Author's Note
From My Heart to Yours

Dear Warrior of Faith,
If you are reading this, it means you showed up day after day, prayer after prayer, step by step. From the deepest place in my heart, thank you.

When God placed the vision for Holy Rise Up within me, I did not know how deeply it would speak into the lives of those ready to stand, lead, and walk in faith. It is a call to obedience when it costs, to keep moving forward when the path is hard, and to grow under God's direction.

These pages were shaped through real battles and real surrender, written not from above you, but beside you, for the man God is forming you to be.

My prayer is simple. That you would not just read these words, but live them. That your faith would deepen, your trust in God would grow steady, and your life would reflect the purpose placed within you.

Remember this. You are rooted in truth, refined by God's hand, and becoming exactly who you were created to be. No matter how loud the world grows, the foundation beneath you will hold, because it was built by the One who never fails.

Thank you for walking this road with me. For standing firm. For choosing faith. For proving that God is still shaping strong men who rise with conviction and lead with humility.

Stand tall. Stay faithful. Keep rising.

With strength and faith,
Kelley McConnell
Crossroad to Healing
Rooted in Truth. Forged in Faith. Rising in Victory.

A Note from Kelley:

If this devotional has strengthened your faith, sharpened your resolve, or helped you stand more firmly in God's truth, I would genuinely love to hear from you. Your reflections, testimonies, and reviews help this message reach more men and boys who are ready to rise, stand strong, and walk boldly in their faith.

If you feel led, please take a moment to leave a short review on Amazon. It matters more than you may realize and helps place this book into the hands of those who need encouragement, clarity, and courage for the road ahead.

And if you'd like to share your Holy Rise Up journey on Instagram, tag @crossroadtohealing, @HolyGlowUp365 and use the hashtag #HolyRiseUp so we can stand together, celebrate growth, and honor the work God is doing in and through your life.

With gratitude and faith,

Kelley

About the Author
Kelley McConnell

Kelley McConnell is the founder of Crossroad to Healing, a Christ-centered wellness ministry dedicated to helping individuals restore mind, body, and spirit through faith, biblical truth, and holistic alignment with God's design.

A visionary practitioner, mentor, and author, Kelley is also the creator of the IASIS Healing Method, a Christ-centered, Spirit-led approach that supports deep restoration and alignment with God's design for wholeness. Through IASIS and her RESTORE Nutritional Healing program, she has guided countless individuals toward renewed strength, purpose, and spiritual vitality.

Kelley's writing journey began with Holy Glow-Up: 365 Days to Shine from Within, a devotional created to guide women through healing, renewal, and restoration in Christ. As her work expanded, so did her calling to encourage strength, discipline, and spiritual leadership in the next generation. Holy Rise Up was written as a companion devotional, designed to equip boys and men to stand firm in truth, grow in character, and rise boldly into the purpose God has placed on their lives.

Her writing blends faith, strength, and encouragement, challenging readers to grow in integrity, endurance, and obedience. Kelley believes true transformation happens when healing and purpose work together, producing lives rooted in Christ and lived with courage.

When she is not creating, teaching, or writing, Kelley can often be found grounding in nature, spending time with her family, or serving others through everyday acts of faithfulness. She believes true strength is built through surrender to God, and that every boy and man carries a divine calling waiting to be fully lived out.